SALMON
&
WOMEN

Recordbreakers of the future? Sarah (left) and Juliet Wood, twin great-granddaughters of A. H. E. Wood, most formidable of 20th-century salmon anglers. His portrait hangs at Fishmongers' Hall in the City of London. Sarah is the more enthusiastic fisher of the twins.

SALMON
&
WOMEN
The Feminine Angle

Wilma Paterson
and Professor Peter Behan
(Dept of Neurological Sciences, University of Glasgow)

INTRODUCTION by HUGH FALKUS

*"Angling may be said to be so like the
Mathematicks, that it can never be fully learnt;
at least not so fully, but that there will still be
more new experiments left for the trial of other
men that succeed us...."*

Izaak Walton
The Compleat Angler

H. F. & G. WITHERBY LTD

AUTHOR'S NOTE

I would like to thank all the women who took the time to talk to me about their fishing experiences, and also all the men (husbands, sons, grandsons, friends, gillies) who put me in touch with them. Sadly it was impossible to follow up all the many leads and there will, I fear, be many omissions in this book. But I hope that this modest sample will suffice to demonstrate the extraordinary success that women have had in salmon fishing over the last hundred years.

My thanks also to taxidermist Alan Allison for his help and interest, and for confiding to me the names of ladies whose husbands, fathers, fathers-in-law, etc, had commissioned casts of large fish caught by them; to the Morison family of Mountblairy for their kindness in lending precious photographs of Mrs Morison and most especially to the Reverend Routledge Bell, former Minister of Caputh Parish and friend of Miss Georgina Ballantine for 35 years, for his invaluable help and generosity.

W.P.

First published in Great Britain 1990 by
H. F. & G. WITHERBY LTD
14 Henrietta Street, London WC2E 8QJ

© Wilma Paterson and Peter O. Behan 1990
Introduction © Hugh Falkus 1990

The right of Wilma Paterson and Peter Behan to be identified
as authors of this work has been asserted by them in accordance
with the Copyright, Designs and Patents Act 1988.

British Library Cataloguing in Publication Data
Paterson, Wilma
  Salmon and women: the feminine angle.
  1. Angling
  I. Title   II. Behan, Peter O.
  799.1755

  ISBN 0–85493–201–1

Designed by John Grain

Printed and bound in Great Britain by
Butler & Tanner Ltd, Frome and London

Contents

Hugh Falkus with his wife Kathleen. 'Often, when I can't catch fish, she can, and does!'

Introduction

During the 1920s, women anglers established three British salmon records that have not been beaten.

From the Tay in October, 1922, Miss Georgina Ballantine landed a fish of 64 lb, the biggest ever caught on rod and line. From the Deveron in October, 1924, Mrs Clementina Morison landed the fly-caught record: a 61-pounder. From the Wye on 12 March, 1923, Miss Doreen Davey caught the record spring fish of $59\frac{1}{2}$ lb. In that decade, British rivers provided women anglers with at least two other exceptional fish: a 55-pounder by Mrs Gladys Huntington from the Awe on 19 September, 1927, and a 50-pounder from the Tay at Kinnaird by Miss Lettice Ward on 12 October, 1928.

At the time the capture of these monsters aroused a lot of interest. What seemed extraordinary then (and still does) was that such a tiny minority of women salmon fishers could account for so many of the biggest fish landed.

Their success during the 1930s continued to surprise. Fishing Tweed for a day in 1935, Lady Joan Joicey made the remarkable catch of 26 salmon and two sea trout. It was merely one among many notable bags by women anglers, achieved while 'Jock Scott' (the pen-name of D. G. F. Rudd) was preparing the manuscript of his book: *Game Fish Records* (H. F. & G. Witherby, 1936). Puzzled by the statistics, he wrote: 'I have often wondered why ladies prove to be so exceptionally successful at salmon fishing ... The luring of sixty pounders appears to be a lost art amongst male anglers in the British Isles, or can it be that ultra-large salmon prefer being caught by ladies? *Quién sabe?* Whatever secret feminine anglers possess, it is, judging by results, a very potent one, and I wish I could discover it!' Unwittingly, 'Jock Scott' may have stumbled on an astonishing possibility: that there really *was* a secret. As this book suggests, although most people in the angling world would be prepared nowadays to attribute women's success either to luck or skill, or both, there may be yet another cause. *Salmon and Women* approaches it from two standpoints: The scientific and the philosophical.

First, the scientific. Prompted by an hypothesis relating to feeding and non-feeding mechanisms of the salmon suggested by my friend Dr David Goldsborough and published in my book *Salmon Fishing*, Professor Peter Behan of Glasgow University has been researching the condition known as anorexia – a not uncommon starvation syndrome which affects humans and can be fatal. During the course of his experiments, Peter Behan became deeply interested in the salmon's amazing capacity to smell and taste, those remarkable senses that guide a fish back from the sea to its natal river. Was it possible that the big male salmon often caught by women at the back-end of the season could actually sense the stimulating proximity of a female angler?

Social communication among fish – controlling dominance, sexual behaviour and aggression – is achieved through the chemical messages of pheromones: substances given off in scent, usually from the skin, which can affect the behaviour of other animals not necessarily of the same species. It is known that salmon can detect water-borne chemical messages to an astonishing degree. For instance, the odours of a man's hand will sometimes repel or alarm salmon, whereas those of a woman's hand will not. A first-hand account of this phenomenon (no pun intended) comes from Mr Garry Hewitt of Lewiston, Idaho, USA: 'When I heard about this I finally understood something that occurred on the Clear-water River, Idaho, back in 1966. The man counting the fish passing the Portlatch Dam claimed that he could stop salmon and steelhead trout from entering the dam's fish ladder by merely putting one finger into the water at the top of the ladder. He said he didn't like to do this very often because it would keep fish out of the ladder for as long as thirty minutes, delaying fish passage.

'One day when friends and I were visiting the dam, just as the fish counter was about to demonstrate his finger trick the only woman in our group volunteered to do it.

'When she put her finger into the water at the head of the ladder, upstream from the observation window, the fish continued to swim past the window without any sign of agitation. The fish counter told her to put her entire hand into the water and swish it back and forth. She did this for about a minute. The fish took no notice.

'Then the fish counter went to the head of the ladder, to the same place where the woman was, put *one finger* into the water and for about ten seconds swished it to and fro. A few seconds later the fish in the observation window became extremely agitated. Then they turned tail and swam back down the ladder.

'At that, all of us went up on top where we could observe the lower part of the ladder. All over the place downstream, fish were jumping out of the water in panic.

'The fish counter had no explanation why the woman's hand hadn't frightened the fish. Of course, at that time no one knew anything about chemical communication.

'Today I always wash my hands before going fishing. I even wash before a session of fly-tying to keep my flies "uncontaminated". When I do this I find that I can catch trout almost as well as my wife!'

That salmon might respond to women via the female pheromones is a theory yet to be proved, but some scientists think it not unlikely. To quote the famous Norwegian biologist, Professor Doving: 'It is quite possible that salmon can sense the sex hormones of women and become attracted to them, even if these come in minute quantities on an angling lure.' Professor Behan's examination of this possibility comprises the second part of this book.

The further line of enquiry is a discussion with a large number of successful female anglers about their methods and opinions. By many of the ladies interviewed, the suggestion that there could be a scientific explanation of their success was greeted with scepticism and amusement. Some thought it a conspiracy of male chauvinists, bad losers to a man, who were prepared to attribute female superiority in a predominantly masculine sport to a form of witchcraft rather than to skill and dedication.

But what, non-salmon-fishing readers may reasonably ask, is so remarkable about catching salmon either big or small? Why so much fuss?

For their benefit, and for the full appreciation of the stories recounted in this book, I should explain that salmon are migratory fish: they hatch and spend the first couple of years or so of their lives in the fresh water of a river, after which they go to sea, feed avidly for a period varying between one and three or four years, then return to the river as adults to mate and spawn. But what makes the sport of salmon fishing so special is that on their return from sea salmon *stop feeding*. A casual onlooker, therefore, might be forgiven for regarding the hooking of these fish as something of an esoteric rite in which sorcery must of necessity play a major part.

Extraordinary though it may be, however, although the returning salmon take no further food they will sometimes, inexplicably, take an angler's bait or lure. Why? Nobody knows. Many hypotheses have been advanced but none has been proved. Small wonder then that, to an outsider, anyone fishing for salmon with rod and line must be slightly deranged. After all, who but a simpleton would *expect* to hook a fish that, while lying in the river waiting to spawn, has no appetite, lives on the supply of nourishment stored in its tissues and has no need of food? What is surprising is not that salmon are hard to catch, but that any are caught at all. Why should this non-feeding fish ever take *any* sort of bait or lure?

And of course during most of the time we cast to them they *won't* take. Salmon frequently seem impossible to catch. They just lie there, refusing everything on offer – until suddenly, one of them will treat our offering like a long-awaited snack and half-swallow it. Or – as if this behaviour were not by itself sufficiently surprising and illogical – a fish will suck the thing in and puff it out again, or tweak it, or chin it, or slap it with his tail, or roll on it (if it's lying on the bottom), or half-take it, stand-on-end and balance it on his nose. I have watched salmon do all of these things.

It is an axiom of hunters that to be successful they must learn to think like the creatures they hunt. When salmon are the quarry, the humorist who said: 'You don't have to be crazy to go fishing, but it helps', was nearer the truth than he probably imagined. The salmon is a crazy fish and to excel as a salmon angler one has to be, if not raving, at least shall we say infinitely flexible in one's approach.

Is it surprising, then, that the success rate of women is so high? They are, after all, built on rather different lines from men.

Don't misunderstand me. Not for a moment am I implying that female anglers are *madder* than male anglers, merely that they have a different way of seeing things. They are, I suggest, more capable of adapting to crazy situations. Once seized with the lust for salmon they fish with utter determination – especially if there are men fishing the water too. Nothing diminishes their concentration. Foul weather will not discourage them, nor physical discomfort quench their spirit. Whatever the chances they will stick it out, refusing to be beaten, and I have known only darkness drive them from the river. Years ago, in my B.B.C. television film *Salmo the Leaper*, following a sequence when my host's wife comes in with two fish to my one, I wrote: 'Often enough the women will beat the men ... I put it down to their sheer dogged persistence. Once they start fishing they simply will not give up.' You think I exaggerate? Listen. Have you ever tried sharing a rod with a woman for a day on a salmon beat? I have. I spent the first half-hour teaching her the rudiments of Speycasting – and the rest of the day gillying. Take my advice, if you want to do any fishing yourself, *always* arrange for two rods. Once her claws curl round that cork grip you will never get it back. Sharing is over for the day ... What's that? ... You must be joking. Just you try prizing those fingers loose. Whisking round the house with vacuum cleaners gives women very strong wrists – one reason why they make such good Speycasters.

Needless to say, this advice is aimed at my male readers. Members of the fairer sex will not if they are sensible ever dream of sharing a rod – if only to avoid the tears when they catch the only fish of the day.

Just in case you think I'm going adrift in my old age, let me assure you that if my life were at stake I would fish salmon against anybody, male or female; but if Fate demanded a team match, I would unhesitatingly choose a team of women.

This choice is founded on women's willingness to learn. Years of teaching salmon fishing and Speycasting have convinced me that a lot of men – successful businessmen in particular – just hate the idea of having lessons. Even the thought of 'going back to school' is anathema (although, my word! From what I see on my travels, most of them could profit from some casting tuition!) Women, on the other hand, *seek* good advice and usually act on it. Mr Eddie McCarthy, Fishery Superintendent of the River Thurso, is very interesting on this point: 'Women are much more attentive and 90% easier to teach than men. What's more, they retain what they have been taught better than men do. Women have a very strong competitive spirit and they want to outdo the men, probably because as anglers most men don't take them seriously ...'

After all this it comes as no surprise to find that the first angling book printed in English: *A Treatyse of Fysshynge wyth an Angle* is attributed to a woman: Dame Juliana Berners. Published in 1496, after the manuscript had been copied by monks in 1450, it was probably written c. 1425. And a very good book it is.

Yes, I know. The feminine authorship has been pooh-poohed. But not by me. Having studied the book I am a firm believer in Dame Juliana. And indeed, why not? Women can do it today. Why not then?

There have been many women who could fish as well as any men, and better than most. That their exploits have not received more publicity may be due simply to male chauvinism. The King of Fish represents the pinnacle of many a man's hunting prowess. There is, perhaps, something atavistic in his desire to prove his manhood, proudly to exhibit the spoils of the chase to an admiring wife and family – as many cave paintings and drawings suggest has been done since human time began. Besides, some examples come from the years during two world wars, when there was scant news space for details of wealthy women angling in safe luxury on remote northern rivers.

It must not be thought, however, that tales of feminine success belong only to the distant past. Here is a note from my old mate Arthur Oglesby: 'Concerning your quest to relate the capture of big salmon to the female species. In Norway, on the opening day of the 1984 season, Toril Haraldsen was fishing the Vossö. She started at around 10 and packed up just before dinner. During that time she hooked and landed 10 salmon *averaging 37 lb. The biggest went to 53 lb!* It was considered to be the best catch of salmon ever made by a woman. Certainly it is the most noteworthy catch I have ever heard about by a woman – or a man, for that matter.'

Another intriguing first-hand account comes from Asbjörn Fiva, one of Norway's finest all-round fly-fishers and sportsmen. Raised on the banks of the Rauma river in the beautiful Romsdal valley, he was an expert salmon fisher by the age of 15 and worked for some years as a gillie on the superb Bromley Davenport water. Among regular visitors to the river was a couple from Oslo. Invariably, both in size and number, the wife's catch of salmon was bigger than her husband's. When it was suggested to Asbjörn recently that this may have been due to the lady's pheromones, he replied: 'I like your English humour, but I can easily tell you why the lady always caught more fish than the gentleman: it was because she always did everything I tell her. She put on the fly that I advised, she cast the fly in the place I suggested, and if I suggested something else she did it without question. You see, I know my river. I know all the lies where the fish take. All she had to do was to cover them correctly. The gentleman was too clever an angler, too proud to accept advice. He followed his own ideas and caught little or nothing. If there were fish in the river, the lady caught them.'

The ability of women to beat the men on the same day in the same water occurs time and again. The following example appeared not long ago in an article for *Country Life*, by that keen sportsman Max Hastings, editor of the *Daily Telegraph*: 'Women, when they choose, are often better fishers than men – perhaps they possess a more highly developed sense of rhythm. But I suspect that many take up a rod only in self-defence, in order to make the best of it when their husbands insist upon an annual migration to Scotland ... My own wife will happily cast a fly if we are together on a salmon river, and a year or two ago much enjoyed hooking two salmon in 10 minutes on a day that I could do nothing.

'I do not think she would regard it as a great deprivation if she was told that she could never fish again. But it is infinitely agreeable for any woman to demonstrate that, when she chooses, she can wipe the eye of lesser (male) mortals. Among Barbara Cartland's many qualities, determination and courage rank high. There was a story of her on the Helmsdale a few years ago, mercilessly teasing the men in her party every evening in the lodge about their inability to catch fish in bright sunshine and low water.

'One of them, supremely provoked, was rash enough to mutter something about: "Well, I'd like to see you do any better." The next morning, the pink Rolls-Royce bore the prodigious novelist majestically to the riverside. A few casts later, she hooked her fish. Ten minutes on, the triumphant procession returned in state to the lodge, having made its point. That is show business for you.'

It certainly is. But more, much more than that is Barbara Cartland's sublime display of confidence. The biology of the salmon being what it is, she was on a beating to nothing. But she triumphed. In salmon fishing, absolute confidence is probably the most valuable asset of all.

And so, as Kipling might have written: 'Let us now praise famous women'! By any standards their angling history is astonishing – as testified by the examples in this fascinating book. Pheromones my foot! As Kipling *did* write: 'The female of the species is more deadly than the male'! Whatever chemical messages may be washing about down there in the water, women, I feel sure, need no hormonal help in hooking salmon.

HUGH FALKUS
Cragg Cottage
1990

P.S. Mind you, one of these days there'll be some red faces if we're all proved wrong!

PART ONE

SOME ACHIEVEMENTS OF FEMALE ANGLERS

'My God – it's a woman!'

Gillie on Deeside after arriving too late to help Margaret Emmott
land a 24 lb salmon. March 1985.

TO-DAY'S
PERTHSHIRE
ADVERTISER

UPKEEP OF COUNTY ROADS
MOTOR TRAFFIC PROBLEM

LOGIERAIT POORHOUSE
THE QUESTION OF CLOSING

Monster Salmon Caught in Tay
CAPUTH LADY'S TUSSLE

ALYTH PARISH CHURCH WAR MEMORIAL

Latest District News

FOOTBALL IN THE COUNTY

The Tay at Caputh. Glendelvine Water. In October 1922, this was the scene of the most famous battle in the history of salmon fishing.

Record-Breakers

Losh, Miss Ballantine! Hoo I envye yon saxty-fower poonder!
I wush
That whether on minny or fly, I could fickle sae michty a fush!
I can fancy the scene on that day, your feyther and you at the
stell
The pule on the glorious Tay, the Autumn wund bladdy and
snell:
Gulls and teuchits and ducks i' the sky, the grey-lags (the first
this back-end)
The goosander's sad cry as the watter rins by, the rise i' the run
at the bend!
The rugg! 'He has ta'en it fell weel! The line's rinnin' ootward
like wud!'
The bonnie wee lilt o' the reel! 'Noo lassie mind hud up yer rod!'
He's plouterin' hither and yon! He's warsellin' doon tae the
burn!
He's loupin' like onything mon! 'Noo canny, and redd up the
pirn!'
Twa hoors and a hauff tae the grass! yon lassie is wearit, nae
doot:
But here's tae yon lass! Awa' fill yer glass! The whole fushin'
world follys suit!

attributed to Bobby Band of the Glendelvine syndicate

NOTE: fickle *deceive*; stell *a pool or salmon lie in the river*; bladdy *gusty*; snell *chill*; teuchits *lapwings*; rugg *a strong pull*; like wud *like mad*; plouterin' *floundering*; warsellin' *struggling*; loupin' *zigzagging*; redd up the pirn *retrieve the line taken from the reel*

MISS BALLANTINE

One Saturday evening in October 1922 a young woman called Georgina Ballantine was in her father's boat, fishing the Glendelvine water of the River Tay when suddenly there was a 'rug' and a screech of the reel. She didn't know it at the time but she had just hooked the biggest salmon ever taken on rod and line in Great Britain. The fish weighed 64 lb and Miss Ballantine's record is unlikely now ever to be surpassed.

Georgina was the daughter of James Ballantine, fisherman to Alexander Lyle of Glendelvine estate, and the two of them, both keen anglers, had taken advantage of the Laird's indisposition to take the day's rods. By tea time Miss Ballantine had already caught three good-sized salmon (25, 21 and 17 lb) but because it was nearing the end of the season and the clocks would be going back that night they decided to continue fishing until dusk. It was 6.15 pm when Miss Ballantine's monster fish was hooked in the stream above the Bargie Stone and the thrilling battle which followed lasted two hours and five minutes.

Shortly afterwards Miss Ballantine wrote an account of the struggle which P. D. Malloch (who supplied the tackle which brought the salmon within reach of the 'gaffer') sent to the *Fishing Gazette*. It was published in the issue of 21 October, 1922, and not since, to my knowledge, so I think it merits reprinting here in full.

> LANDING OF THE RECORD TAY SALMON
> On the evening of 7 October, 1922, after a rather strenuous day's fishing, which resulted in the capture of three fine salmon, we determined to finish the day on the river. It was the last evening before the hour changed, therefore we were anxious to make the most of our time.
> We amounted to Father and myself, he rowing, as Melvin,

the boatman, had knocked off at 5 pm. After towing up
the boat we started harling, using two rods, the fly
'Wilkinson' on the right, and the dace, which I was plying
on the left. The bait was exceptionally well put on with an
attractive curl on its tail and spinning along briskly as only
Malloch's minnows can spin.

A few turns at the top of 'Boat Pool' as the sun dipped
down behind the hill brought no result. Immediately above
the 'Bargie' stone Father remarked that we should 'see him
here': scarcely were the words spoken when a sudden 'rug'
and 'screech' of the reel brought my rod in an upright
position. He was hooked! The bait he seized with no
unusual violence at 6.15 pm and thinking him an ordinary-
sized fish, we tried to encourage him to play into the back
water behind 'Bargie', a large boulder. Our hopes, however,
upon this point were soon 'barkin' and fleein''. Realizing
evidently that something was amiss, he made a headlong
dash for freedom and flew (I can apply no other term to
his sudden flight). Down the river he went in mid-stream,
taking a run of about 500 yards before stopping, at the
same time carrying with him about 150 yards of line. Quick
as lightning the boat was turned, heading down-stream,
and soon we overtook and got him under hand and within
reasonable distance.

Heading for the north bank, we were in the act of landing
about 200 yards above the Bridge when he came practically
to the end of the boat.[1] Scenting danger ahead, he again
ran out of reach. Leaving the boat, we followed him down,
and as chance would have it he passed between the north
pier and the bank when going under the Bridge,[2] otherwise

[1] Had a third party been at hand he might have been gaffed within ten
minutes.
[2] Bridge has two piers, three divisions.

we would have been in a dreadful hole.

Not once did he show himself, so we were mercifully kept in blissful ignorance of the monster we were fated to fight to the death.

About 200 yards below the Bridge Father thought it advisable to fetch the boat, as the fish obstinately kept out in the current. Evidently our progress downstream was farther than Father had anticipated, as I immediately got into hot water; 'dinna lat the beast flee doon the watter like that, 'ummin'.

With few remarks and much hand-spitting[1] we again boarded the boat, this time keeping in mid-stream for fully half an hour. As time went on the strain of this was getting beyond us; the fish remained stationary and sulked. Then we endeavoured to humour and encourage him to the Murthly bank, but he absolutely refused to move.

Again gradually crossing the river we tried to bring him into the backwater at the junction half-way down to Sparrowmuir, where a small break-water juts out. Again no luck attended our movements in this direction, though we worked with him for a considerable time. Eventually we re-crossed over close to the island. By this time darkness had come down, and we could see the trees on the island silhouetted against the sky.

We had hoped by the light of the moon to find a suitable landing-place, but unfortunately a dark cloud obscured her. The fish kept running out a few paces, then returning, but long intervals were spent without even a movement. He inclined always downstream, until the middle of the island was reached, and the light in the cottage window at Sparrowmuir blinked cheerily across the river.

---

[1] An unconscious habit of Father's when excited.

By this time my left arm ached so much with the weight of
the rod that it felt paralysed, but I was determined that
whatever happened nothing would induce me to give in.
'Man if only the Laird or the Major had ta'en him I
wouldna' ha' been sae ill aboot it.' Encouraging remarks
such as those I swallowed silently. Once I struck the nail
on the head by remarking that if I successfully grassed this
fish he must give me a new frock. 'Get ye the fish landed
first and syne we'll see aboot the frock', was the reply.
(Nevertheless I have kept him to his word and the frock
has been ordered.) By this time we were prepared to spend
the night on the Island.

Tighter, and tighter still, the order came, until the tension
was so great that no ordinary line could have stood the
test for any length of time. It says much for both line and
tackle in playing such an important part. Nearer and nearer
he came until I was ordered to change my seat to the bow
of the boat, and by keeping the rod upright Father was
thus enabled to feel with the gaff the knot at the junction
of line and cast. Having gauged the distance, the remainder
was easy, I wound the reel steadily until only the cast (length
of cast, $3\frac{3}{4}$ yards) was left. One awful moment of suspense
followed – then the gaff went in successfully, which brought
him to the side of the boat. A second lift (no small weight,
over $\frac{1}{2}$ cwt) brought him over the end into the floor of the
boat, Father, out of puff, half sitting on top of him.
Reaching for Mr Moir's 'Nabbie', I made a somewhat
feeble attempt to put him out of pain, and was afterwards
accused of 'knockin' oot ane o' the puir beast's een!' It is
unnecessary to describe the homeward journey; I was
ordered to remain in the boat while Father towed it up.
We were met at the Bridge by the old lady, my mother,
who was considerably relieved to see us back; her greeting

showed how perturbed and anxious she had been during our absence; 'Guid sakes I thocht ye were baith i' the watter!'

No time was lost in administering a stiff dose of 'toddy' which I considered a necessary and well-earned 'nightcap'. Thus ended a 'red-letter' day in the annals of the famous Glendelvine beat of the River Tay.

Miss Ballantine became famous overnight and newspapers all over Britain reported her achievement with every detail of the great fish, which was a fresh-run cock with sea-lice still adhering to its tail. People came from far and near to view the monster. The Laird decided to present it to the patients and staff of Perth Royal Infirmary, but it was first sent to Malloch's of Perth to have a cast made. This was the shop which had supplied the fatal tackle, and Miss Ballantine chanced to pass by on the Monday after the event. A big crowd was gathered around Malloch's window and she thought at first that there had been an accident. But instead, there was her fish on display in the window with a notice stating its weight and that it had been caught by Miss Ballantine:

> 'Nae woman ever took a fish like that oot of the watter,
> mon', she heard one old man say to another, 'it would
> need a horse, a block and tackle, tae tak a fish like that oot.
> A woman – that's a lee anyway.'

Miss Ballantine was shy in the company of strangers or in large gatherings, and she found no pleasure in boasting of her angling prowess. A month or two after her great day she went to see friends in Greenock and found that the local anglers had arranged a dinner and whist drive in her honour at the Tontine Hotel. The fishermen were longing to hear a first-hand account of the battle but Miss Ballantine preferred to delegate this task to her cousin

Miss Ballantine with her father and the record fish, 64 lb.

Mr Cadenhead who delivered a graphic account. The evening anyway was a great success, and Miss Ballantine received many congratulations and a large box of chocolates. The Greenock anglers were particularly gratified to note that among the more enthusiastic of the company were their womenfolk who had hitherto regarded angling with indifference or ill-concealed hostility.

Life was never the same again for Miss Ballantine after that fish. She was now a celebrity, and Victoria Cottage where she lived with her parents became a Mecca for anglers from all over the world. Often credited with catching her record salmon at the tender age of 18 or 20 she was actually 32 at the time and had a distinguished career as a wartime nursing sister behind her. She was decorated for her work for the Red Cross in France and also nursed in hospitals in Perth and London between 1914 and 1919. An enthusiastic all-round sportswoman, Miss Ballantine was a keen bowler and a crack shot at the miniature rifle range, scoring a 'possible' more than once. Fishing however was her great love – she had caught her first salmon at the age of eight – and apart from her service abroad she spent all her days on the banks of her beloved Tay at Victoria Cottage just above the Caputh bridge which had been completed in November 1888, exactly one year before she was born.

James Ballantine had been the ferryman at Caputh, responsible for carrying passengers between the Murthly and Stormont districts of Perthshire. He held a feudal lease, paying a rent for the right to run the ferry and was also under obligation to the estate tenants and to Sir Alexander Muir Mackenzie who owned it. (Mackenzie had actually bought it because of the salmon netting rights that were attached to it and which had originally belonged to the Church.) With the ferry lease came Mr Ballantine's cottage, no more than a 'but and ben' in those days, and a long strip of a croft of about five acres. Obviously there were frequent occasions when storms and bad weather made even such a short crossing impossible, so eventually in 1887 a bridge was proposed to commemorate the Queen's Jubilee. It was named Victoria Bridge and was opened a year later to the general delight of the people of the area.

Victoria Bridge made a huge impact on the daily lives of the people of Caputh and Murthly and was welcomed on all sides, but James Ballantine was now out of a job and looking for something other than his small croft to occupy his time.

Fairly soon however he took charge of the Glendelvine fishings, and so from an early age his daughter learned to fish. Any day that there was no rod from the house, she was sure to be in the boat.

For well over 20 years Miss Ballantine 'looked after' a group of businessmen with fishings on the Tay, all members of a syndicate which rented the Glendelvine and Murthly Castle stretches of the river. They would meet in her garden hut or in the cosy sitting room, where she would provide them with tea or as often as not, a dram. Her hospitality was prodigious and she would sometimes get through three bottles of whisky a week – not taking it herself.

Life was physically very hard for her and the arthritis which was later to cripple her set in early. Her grand-nephew Fergus Morrison remembers his Aunt Ina's hands being claw-like in the 1950s and as early as 1922, in the famous portrait of Miss Ballantine with that enigmatic expression on her face, and her left hand in her jacket pocket, there's a hint of deformity in her right. Victoria Cottage, for all its charm, was a primitive place, with no electricity, only paraffin lamps and a hand pump in the poky kitchen for the water. Latterly Miss Ballantine had to pump the water using her elbows, making even the preparation of a pot of tea a major feat.

If her fisher friends and visitors were unaware of the pain their heroine endured so stoically, they did undoubtedly appreciate her friendship and hospitality, and in 1955 the anglers got together to do something special for her by way of a thank you, and they had her house wired, provided heating and lighting and a generator in an outhouse. There was a grand party to celebrate the switch-on that December, with the anglers and their wives,

Lady Lyle of Glendelvine, the local bobby and minister, the boatmen from Glendelvine and Murthly Castle and friends from all over the country. A large bulb illuminated the lawn down to the water's edge and coloured lights under the eaves transformed cottage and garden into an enchanting fairy scene. Champagne flowed and Miss Ballantine cut the cake which was in the shape of a model of the Pitlochry Dam and Power Station. It was a real work of art, with green 'water' flowing over it and a single candle on the central Tower. Miss Ballantine was thrilled with it, and with the fishermen's gesture:

'I don't know what to say,' she said, 'but I know I'll want to live till I'm a hundred now, to enjoy all this.'

The Rev. F. Routledge Bell was distantly related to Miss Ballantine and on his arrival in Caputh their friendship blossomed – she was known as Sandy in the Bell household. Every Friday at 12.30 the minister and the doctor (Neil Morrison) would meet punctually at Victoria Cottage to discuss over coffee or a dram the ins and outs of the relationships of the parishioners and thanks to Sandy's intimate knowledge of the Parish many a faux-pas was avoided. Mr Bell's wife Susan assisted Miss Ballantine in her job as registrar, accompanied her on holidays latterly, and sometimes Sandy would be persuaded to stay at the Manse, because even with electricity Victoria Cottage was still exceedingly primitive. Looking back, the Bells can see that for their friend many of these years were filled with pain and hardship caused by Sandy's arthritis, and that the courage with which she endured it all was magnificent.

The minister and Sandy MacLennan (the bus proprietor) managed to fit up her house with various gadgets to allow her to get in and out of her wheelchair easily, and they even organized a light switch in every room which could be operated from the floor in case she fell. This was to illuminate the emergency light on the roof of Victoria Cottage, which could be seen in the village,

Miss Ballantine in later years. 'Above all she loved the river bank.'

so when someone would phone the minister and say 'There's a red light flashing on Miss Ballantine's cottage, Mr Bell,' help would soon be on hand.

Victoria Cottage has changed little since Miss Ballantine's death. The garden is neat and trim with its clipped beech hedge all around, fruit bushes and topiary work. The emergency light which her friends installed is still in position on the chimney head and the hut, where the fishermen used to meet, stands empty at the side of the house. In the winter of 1989–90 when there was such devastation caused by storms in the Tay valley, Victoria Cottage was once more flooded and its tenant evacuated, and it was quite empty when I was there in April 1990.

James Ballantine had greatly enlarged the original cottage, adding an extension at the back and a substantial upper storey. Miss Ballantine slept in the room above the porch, with a wonderful view of the river, for as long as she was fit to climb the stairs, and after she was crippled she slept downstairs in the little back bedroom.

She never owned the house. Her good friend F. Routledge Bell, 'the poaching minister'[1] as he is affectionately known in these

---

[1] When the Rev. Routledge Bell became minister of Caputh Parish, he took over the lovely old manse and Glebe on the banks of the Tay, and with it, the right to fish for salmon. The minister took full advantage of this attractive perk, so much so in fact, that the Laird began to take exception to it, and to the Rev. Bell's predilection for salmon for breakfast. He challenged the Church's right to the fishing, but when the matter reached the courts, could produce no documentary evidence to substantiate his claim, and so the minister continued to enjoy his morning delicacy.

parts, once approached the Estate with a plan to raise the money for Miss Ballantine to purchase the house, but his application was rejected and the minister will always marvel at the reason given by Lady Lyle: that Victoria Cottage in its charming riverside situation, was 'the first house we come to on our land.' When

The Ballantines' cottage at Caputh.

Miss Ballantine died the croft and cottage did pass to her nephew and he and his family used it regularly for three years. But in due course the Estate imposed so many conditions on the tenancy that the Ballantines moved out.

The Ballantine family had connections with the parish going back hundreds of years. There was a schoolmaster in the 16th century, two were associated with the 1745 uprising of Bonnie Prince Charlie, and some were elders of the church, as was James Ballantine, the last lessee of Caputh Ferry.

There are no longer any Ballantines in Caputh Parish.

Miss Ballantine never married, and if there was romance in her life she kept it to herself (she corresponded for years with a gentleman in New Zealand). The youngest of a family of four children, she did the expected thing which was to stay at home and care for her elderly parents.

Discipline was certainly the keynote of her life. Her upbringing was strict, she had experienced the discipline of nursing in wartime, in her job as registrar and indeed in her sporting life, not least on that memorable day in 1922.

In the last decade of her life Miss Ballantine was almost completely incapacitated by arthritis and eventually had both legs amputated. She bore this ordeal with courage and fortitude and each day she could be seen sitting in her chair by the river ...

> Above all she loved the river bank which was her home, her interest, her single-minded obsession. Not only did she love it for the changing scene, the play of light and colour upon the water, the fish that could be caught ... but surely for the fishermen who pursued her favourite sport ... for her abiding interest was in people and especially people who fished. I am sure that this is why she will be mourned by men and women in all walks of life and every country

in the world, and why for many years to come there will be those who will turn to their children and say ... 'I knew Miss Ballantine, who caught the record salmon ... she was a truly wonderful person'.
(From an obituary given by Rev. Routledge Bell at the funeral of Miss Ballantine in 1970).

It was 23 February, 1934, and the famous men-only Flyfishers Club of Piccadilly was preparing for its annual Jubilee dinner at

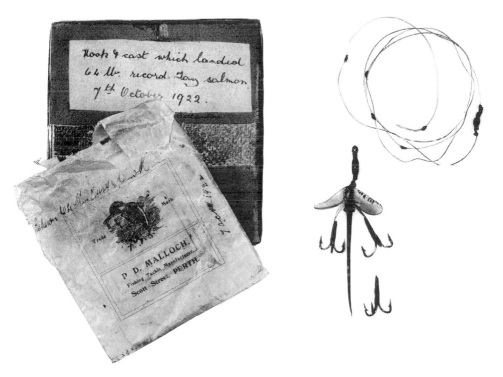

Miss Ballantine's trace and spinning mount, minus 'Dace', on which she took the record salmon.

which Field-Marshal Lord Allenby and Lord Desborough were lined up to speak. Dundee's *Evening Telegraph* sent a young man to report on the forthcoming event and on the club which in 50 years had never dreamed of allowing women to join.

Looking round the premises the reporter was struck by a fine watercolour[1] over the sideboard in the club dining-room, of the record salmon caught in the British Isles, a prodigious looking fish indeed, he thought.

'It weighed 64 lb,' said Major W. H. Saffery, the club's secretary. 'Its length was 54 inches and its girth $28\frac{1}{2}$ inches.'

'Who caught it?' inquired the reporter innocently.

'As a matter of fact,' said Major Saffery in a low voice, 'that fish was caught – by a woman.'

And the heroine of the most titanic salmon battle ever, the one 'fisherman' who could have stretched her arms to their widest extent and still be telling the truth, could not be a member of the famous club!

MRS MORISON
'Dangerously near the mark.'

Miss Ballantine's record Tay salmon was taken on a spinning bait, and there are many anglers who will contend (while in no way wishing to diminish Miss Ballantine's achievement), that this is not quite the same thing as taking one on a fly. As it happens, the biggest fly-caught salmon was also taken by a woman, two years after Miss Ballantine's 64-pounder. She was Mrs Morison of Mountblairy, and the salmon she caught in the Lower Shaw Pool on the Deveron on 21 October, 1924, using a 'Brown Wing Killer', weighed 61 lb, its length $52\frac{1}{2}$ inches and girth 32 inches. It

[1] Painted by J. A. Rennie in its exact size from measurements and an outline supplied to him by Miss Ballantine.

Mrs Morison's 61 lb fish from the Deveron, caught in October 1924, still holds the record for a fly-caught salmon in British waters.

should be mentioned that it was not weighed until 24 hours after it was caught, as the local railway scales were not suitable, and some weight was certainly lost. How much is a matter for speculation, but Mr Harper who attended to the cast in Aberdeen the next day reckoned on a weight loss of a 'pound or two'. 'Dangerously near the mark', in fact, as was scribbled in the margin of Miss Georgina Ballantine's copy of *The Fishing Gazette* of 8 November, 1924, which reported the catch.

Known as 'Tiny', Mrs Morison's nickname was acquired not because of her diminutive stature, although she was not a big woman, but as a result of contraction of her Christian name Clementina. On the face of it she and Georgina Ballantine were poles apart, socially speaking at any rate. Mrs Morison, a Stewart from Laithers, who was proud of her connection with Mary, Queen of Scots, lived in a splendid mansion at Mountblairy where shooting and fishing parties were the order of the day, and there was a large staff in attendance. Moreover, Mrs Morison did not have to wait for the Laird to have a headache before she could take a rod to the river, as a substantial stretch of the Deveron was hers for the fishing.

On the day she caught her big fish, Tiny Morison, like Miss Ballantine two years before, had already caught other sizeable fish – two of 16 lb each. (Sim, the keeper, had got one.) She wrote excitedly to her friend Lt. Col. W. Keith, who had lost a large fish in the same pool the year before, reporting the drama, and he described Tiny's achievement as 'magnificent, especially as Mrs Morison is slimly built, and even to hold a fish of this size would be a great physical strain'.

> Well, I had a day out with the fish on Tuesday last [she wrote]. I had two others of 16 lb each before I got him!! One of them fought like a tiger, and took nearly as long as the big one. You remember the fence in the 'Low Shaw

Pool' below the bushes where you lost yours in? I was
fishing there, and Sim (keeper) behind me (he got one also).
I had just said, 'It's dashed funny, Sim, none of us can get
a fish out of this pool' when I saw a huge tail come up a
bit and a boil and the line tighten close into the bank.
He then showed for a little, and remained absolutely still,
till Sim came to me and said 'Is he big?' I said, 'I think he
is fairly large.' He behaved beautifully, and twice slowly
went straight across the pool, and once a little way down,
taking me across the fence and then when out again turned
over, when Sim said, 'He's a big chap, I think.' By this time
Alick was fishing opposite, and seeing me with a fish on
came down. He then attempted a little run up. I was afraid
he was off, but he caved in very quickly. I held on and he
went up and down the side once or twice and Sim took
him the first chance he got. Then we realised how big he
was. I saw that Sim couldn't get him up the bank (he never
moved on the gaff, luckily), so I rushed down and put my
hand in his gills, and together we dragged him up the bank.
He looked enormous lying on the grass. Sim said, 'My
goodness, he is over 50 lb, I believe.' A huge male fish, well
hooked, but a beautiful shape, of course, coloured. I was
truly thankful. I had no idea what a prize he was or I
should have been nervous, and he would have got off; also
a mercy he was so peaceful. I don't suppose I could have
ever held him had he been otherwise.
Alick says, and so does Sim, he could never have realised
he was held at all, and was asleep!
Sim and I dragged him to the hut. Sim went down for the
forester and his pony cart.
He did not take half an hour to get out, and I had on a thin
cast. A $1\frac{1}{4}$ in. 'Brown Wing Killer' fly with which I had the
other two.

When the cart got up with the four at 6.30 (he was on the
bank at 3.20) he weighed 61 lb. Next morning I had him
photographed by Sim's son. They are A1, and when I get
them printed I will send you one or two. We sent him to
Aberdeen by the first train to get a plaster cast made. He
was there met by the fishing-tackle maker, Mr Harper, of
Brown & Co. He weighed him 61 lb, then, 24 hours after,
so he wrote to me and said, 'Your fish must have been
63 lb when grassed, as these specially large fish soon lose
a pound or two.'
He is now being kippered. I am very proud, as you can
imagine.
He is the biggest ever caught on Deveron, I think, either
Dee, Don or Spey, by rod and line. We sent scales to the
Field, also to Mr Wood, as I am awfully curious to know
his age, and if he has ever been up a river before. I believe
they can tell. We averaged three fish a day for the last
fortnight, but the river though large is still clear, many
more will be got, close on ninety, I think; average, I think,
about 18 or 19 lb.

Tiny's husband Alick, Captain Morison of Bognie and
Mountblairy, was also a formidable fisher, yet he never caught a
salmon over 40 lb. This doesn't appear to have affected their
conjugal felicity though, and their marriage was a very happy
one. Tiny had her sorrows all the same and her areas of vul-
nerability. She probably regretted too, that she had no children
and appears to have been fond of other people's offspring. Her
grand-nephew Gordon, who now owns the estates, showed me a
portrait of the Marquis of Montrose which his Aunt Tiny had
specifically left to him because he had impressed her as a little
boy by one day pointing out to some adults that the portrait *was*
of Montrose and not Charles the Second as most people thought.

After Alick's death Mrs Morison more or less abandoned Mountblairy and settled first of all in Montrose and then in Maryculter near Aberdeen. Her nephew and niece, Gordon and Yvonne Morison, who came over from British Columbia to Mountblairy in 1949, remember her as a very private person and very shy. But she presented an austere front and she ruled her household with a rod of iron. Everything was kept locked up, down to the sugar and flour for baking, and the housekeeper had to account for absolutely everything. But she was wonderfully generous too, and in fact the 'family silver' was in part disposed of during her lifetime – a source of some chagrin to her descendants, who keep a close look-out for the family crest in auctions in the area.

Her niece Yvonne very much enjoyed Aunt Tiny's visits but was grateful for the advance notice which always came, so she could have the house tidy and pristine for the occasion. Not that Mrs Morison would ever have uttered a critical remark, but Yvonne felt she'd notice if there was a bit of dust about.

Mrs Morison would come from Aberdeen by car, and as soon as she stepped out, she would invariably press a crumpled packet into Yvonne's hand in which would be a present – an exquisite piece of jewellery, perhaps. Once it was a beautiful Indian diamond ring.

Charles Middleton was the Morisons' chauffeur and although he was only 11 years old when the big fish was caught, he recalls the excitement:

'I remember seeing the fish and it was enormous! They had to get a horse and cart to take it back from the river. There was fish for everyone at that time. The salmon was smoked and we all got a piece of it.'

Mrs Morison didn't give up fishing altogether when Alick died, but doesn't appear to have fished the Deveron much afterwards. Sometimes she went with Watson, the keeper, to the estuary of

the River Ythan at Newburgh to fish for sea trout, and sometimes
with friends to Cruden Bay to fish for flounders in the sea. And
she became, as many people do as they get older, a very keen
gardener.

Gordon Sutherland of Abriachan, who has the impressive cast
of Mrs Morison's fish, spent many happy days at Mountblairy
as a child, and remembers the Morisons as 'solid, plain living,
Scottish county people'. They were definitely not of the pleasure-
seeking cocktail-party and dances type and they devoted themselves wholeheartedly to running their estates, relaxing with
fishing and shooting and other traditional country pursuits. Mrs
Morison was clearly not interested either in the fine malt whisky
(Glendronach) which was (and still is) produced virtually on the
doorstep of their 'other' house, Frendraught.

During her long period of widowhood Tiny Morison became a
member of the Ladies' Club in Aberdeen and she went there every
week with her great friend Miss Ury. The two also had a long
annual holiday in Speyside, but not salmon fishing. Mrs Morison
clearly had no burning ambition to better the record which
she had achieved in her 30s and which still stands to this day.

DOREEN DAVEY

'The Wye is, of course, a rich man's river,' wrote A. Courtney
Williams in 1928, 'drawing room fishing, but wonderful fishing
too ... it is not an easy river to fish, and to be successful the
angler must be skilled. For one thing, long casting is necessary,
and it is frequently essential to throw a Devon minnow – and a
light one at that – for some forty yards. For another, the method
of working a minnow is of great importance and much depends
upon it. . . .'

On the evening of 13 March, 1923, Miss Doreen Davey hooked

a large fish on the Winforton water of the River Wye. At $59\frac{1}{2}$ lb, $52\frac{1}{2}$ inches long and with a girth of 29 inches it broke all previous records (Colonel Tilney had killed a 52-pounder in Higgins Wood at Whitney, in 1920), and the record is still unbroken to this day. It is in fact the heaviest spring fish caught with the rod in Britain.

Young Doreen, daughter of Major G. W. Davey, of Kinnersley Castle, Herefordshire, who owned the Lower Winforton waters, was both enthusiastic and skilled. She had been fishing since the age of five and was with her father when she hooked the big fish. She was using a Hatton aluminium minnow and the fish was hooked in a well-known salmon hole called the 'Cow Pond' at about six in the evening. Thanks to her father's tuition, Miss Davey played the fish with great expertise and received occasional help from him when her arms began to tire.

When the light began to fail, Miss Davey's chauffeur, who also doubled as gaffer, as was often the case in those days, solved the problem by collecting lots of wood and making a bonfire. The salmon put up a tremendous struggle and showed no signs of surrendering for well over an hour. Eventually it was landed at a few minutes to eight, and on examination turned out to be a cock fish, about six years old.

It was exhibited in Hereford next day and attracted a large number of admirers.

'It looked like a massive side of bacon when lying on the slab,' someone recounted at the time.

Miss Davey, who later became Mrs Pryce-Jenkins, wrote a lively account of her battle for the *Fishing Gazette* of 31 March, 1923: 'The attack the large salmon made upon me, my defence, and its ultimate defeat'.

> The story should really begin about six weeks ago, for it was then that my mother suggested that I should go to Biarritz with her. I said I would rather stay here and hunt

with the Radnor and West Hereford Hounds and catch
some salmon. That was the start, for had I gone to Biarritz
I should not have caught my big fish! Then came the day
of the catch. Just as we started walking towards the river
at Winforton, Mr Powell said to me, 'Now, Miss Davey,
you know what you have got to do today! Mr Merton has
just got a forty-five pounder, Mrs Hope has got one about
the same size, and so you have to catch one at least forty-
seven pounds!' Just as I began to fish my father said to me,
'Don't forget. If you hook a "Monster" treat it with just
the same disrespect as you would a twenty-pounder. If you
get anxious and try to favour it you will probably lose it.
That's how the big ones get off!' It was curious how I had
the big ones so impressed on me that day!
The 'Cowpond' begins, I believe, near my father's fishing
hut, and continues downwards for about 200 yards of deep
water with a strong current through it – good fly water
with a rough stony bottom – until it bends into what is
known locally as the 'Middle Hole'. The 'Middle Hole'
always holds fish, but only once in eighteen years has a
salmon been taken there. It is a deep, broad, swirly place,
and the fish run up from it into the 'Cowpond', probably
to discuss the weather, take the air and sometimes, I believe,
to lure the angler! This one did so! I fished over him in the
morning, for my father generally turns me on to the best
places. The salmon was probably thinking of other things
just then – perhaps of his coming honeymoon or of the vile
wind which was blowing, for he would not come and join
in the sport!
I fished all day, as did my father, but nothing would
respond. At about 5.30 p.m., having lost all hope and fully
expecting to have to go home and record another blank
day, I was making a few casts while waiting for my father

Miss Davey and her 59½ lb salmon. 24 March, 1923. A record for the Wye and the heaviest spring fish recorded in the British Isles.

to join me, and I hooked a fish on a small minnow I had put on for a change. I adopted the usual tactics, but the fish just swam about and did more or less what he liked! I believe it is even possible that he growled at me, but a cold north-east wind drowned the noise and so I did not hear it! He had several nice bits of exercise, but he never jumped or let me get a glimpse at him, and I had to do practically what he suggested, for I was unable to make any real impression on him.

After about twenty minutes of this my father came along, and I called to him to take a turn. He put on as much strain as possible, and gave me the rod back again in about ten minutes, saying it was my 'funeral' and so I ought to do the bulk of the work! So I went on again for about ten minutes and then we changed once more and my father did his best to make the fish really annoyed. We did not want him to go down the river any further, and he did not want to go up! We had been taken as far down the river as was safe.

Then we found that we could annoy the salmon best by walking him up the river with very hard pulling, and then running down with him. So we continued doing this as far as we were allowed to do it by the brute. Of course I was constantly varying the angle of the strain, so as to throw him off his balance, but he countered this by varying his position to meet what I was doing. And so it went on, and it grew darker as the twilight faded. I had to fight the daylight as well as the fish! Luckily the fish and the river were west of us and so we could see the line for quite a long time in the twilight.

Then, at last, about seven o'clock, he got quite cross, running down and across the river wallowing along the surface so that we could see him for the first time. Up to now we had only been guessing, but in the fading twilight we could see that it was really a monster reflected on the surface of the water. After this it soon got quite dark, and Jellis, father's chauffeur, had a brain-wave! He has been with us for about twenty years, we call him John, and he has gaffed lots of salmon. He started a large fire on the river bank, and got some paraffin and paper from the hut ready for the crucial moment when the gaff should be required. It was a 'desperate fine battle', but the fish now had to do what we wanted him to do more often than when the fight started. We knew that if the hold was good and the tackle did not give out from the long continued strain, 'beauty would defeat the beast'! An onlooker, who had never caught a fish before, gave us quite an amusing turn. He thought it was about time to pour some of our precious paraffin on the fire, thinking we wanted more light. There was no one to stop him, and he did it. I can smell that funny odour of singed cloth even now!

Then my father swore! He was taking a spell at the rod, and I went to feed the fire. The tin of paraffin had been left near with the cork out, and I accidentally kicked it over! I saved enough for the final effort, however, and father quietened down! We were joined by a fishing neighbour, Mr Barret, and Mr Merton's gillie, Charley Donald, who had come to see what the trouble was about, having noticed the fire and the figures moving about. They brought four inches of candle with them – bless 'em!

The fish, by now, was making shorter journeys, and was 'jagging' badly – a most disquieting action to the angler, for it feels as though every jag must break something! The only safe thing to do, I think, is to keep the top of one's rod well up, and rather easy, allowing the top joint to do what it was intended to do.

The end came with almost dramatic suddenness. The fish
took a few long lunges, rolled a bit, ran, and was pulled
to the right towards the bank. Jellis crept quickly to the
right, but the fish saw him cross the firelight for he jinked,
ran back and round to my left. He was steered in, and, in
a mix-up of splash and spray, the faithful John Jellis with
the gaff and Charley Donald with his hands as much round
the tail of the fish as he could get them managed to haul
him out of the water. The fish was landed at 7.35, and was
hooked at 5.40! One hour and fifty-five minutes of
concentrated excitement and real hard work! We never gave
him a moment's peace, and played him hard the whole
time with the sort of strain that will kill a twenty-pound
fish in seven or eight minutes.

Luckily for us Mr Powell, of Winforton, who kindly allows
us to leave the car with him, formed himself into a 'search
party' and came to look for our corpses with a hurricane
lamp – a thing anyone in our family is warned not to
bother about under three days! However, we were very glad
to see him and his lamp, for we were able to find our way
back to the car. The fish was taken to the office of the Wye
Board of Conservators the next day and was weighed and
measured – weight fifty-nine and a half pounds, length fifty-
two and a half inches, girth twenty-nine inches. The fish
was then displayed in Hereford, an outline for a carving
made, and the flesh was then sold, the proceeds to be given
to the Herefordshire General Hospital.

I have had dozens of nice letters of congratulation from
friends and complete strangers. Amongst the strangers,
some have sent poetry and one proposes that I should marry
him! However, this is another 'catch' and I am not rising!
So many people have written inquiring as to all the tackle,
etc., that I may as well take this opportunity of satisfying

Miss Doreen Davey fishing the Cow Pond where she hooked the record fish.

their curiosity. Reading from left to right, or rather, beginning at the end where the worm fits on! – the minnow was a two inch aluminium of Hattons', Hereford, hook and mount also Hattons'. The line was an old and ridiculously thin undressed silk, supplied by Hattons' to my uncle, Lieut. J. S. Davey, who was killed at Ypres in 1914. This line killed a thirty-four-pounder in 1914, so you can tell that it was a good bit of stuff. The rod was a split cane made by someone many years ago who didn't know his job! Perhaps that is why my father gave it to me! But Mr Hatton has it periodically to make the joints good, and it looks quite all right and ready for another! The reel was a 'Rolo', which I like immensely, and was a Christmas present from my father.

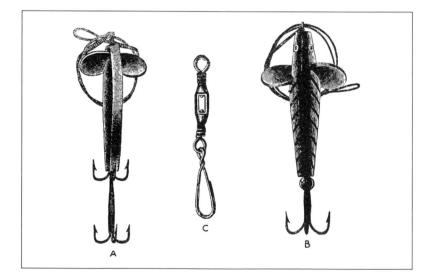

A. and B.: Types of Devon Minnow used on the Wye; C.: Link Swivel.

Now with regard to 'the fool at the other end'! I started to
fish when I was five years of age. That was with a bread
pill for a roach in competition with my father. He used to
beat me then. Now, as the Americans say, I have him cold!
My father takes tens in boots, smokes Franklyn's Shag and
has a catapult in his pocket except when he goes to London,
which is not often!

I only once hooked a bigger fish and that was when we
were trolling for pollack in Basentarbot Bay, on the west
coast of Scotland. It stopped the boat! The skipper shouted
'Hard a-starboard' but father went hard a-port, as it was
more natural to him! That fish said 'Good-bye' and I must
say 'Good-bye' too, but not before thanking all my friends
and correspondents for their very kind congratulations. I
am indeed lucky!

H.M. The Queen Mother when Duchess of York, fishing in New Zealand, 1927. (See page 130.)

Exceptional Bags

'I have witnessed enough incidents when men have had their eyes wiped by "mere women" to wonder whether the Big Fisherman in the Sky looks upon the female of the species with an especially kindly eye.'

Douglas Sutherland, *The Salmon Book*, 1982

GLADYS BLANCHE HUNTINGTON

On 19 September, 1927, Gladys Huntington hooked a huge fish in the Erracht Pool of the river Awe. The four-hour struggle which followed was epic and exhausting, not surprisingly since the fish was hooked in the back, between the head and the dorsal fin. It was finally gaffed in deep water by her gillie wading up to his waist in the Fishing Field almost a mile downstream from where it was hooked, and both angler and fish were utterly worn out by this time. It was a red cock fish of 55 lb and, interestingly, it was probably never revealed in public that Mrs Huntington's fish was hooked 'outside the mouth' or even on a prawn because it was photographed with a fly beside it!

Gladys Huntington's career was a relatively short one, less than 25 years; in that time she caught around 300 fish including a 49-pounder on a prawn in Brander Pool on the Awe in 1933, not long before she died at the age of 53. It was after her marriage to Major Arthur Huntington that Gladys became really interested in fishing and she caught her first fish, a 6 lb grilse, on the Awe in

Gladys Blanche Huntington took a 55 lb salmon from the Awe in September 1927.

1909 on a small trout rod. The same week she landed a 12 lb salmon and she ended her first season with eight fish to her rod.

It was not until 1918 that the Huntingtons bought part of the river Awe in Argyllshire, so Gladys's early experience was of various rivers – the Spey, Wye, Dee, Deveron and Beauly – besides the Awe. She became an expert flyfisher early in her career and threw a long line Speycasting with a greenheart rod. The Green Highlander was probably her most successful fly, but Silver Doctor, Mar Lodge and Wilkinson all feature strongly in the Huntington fishing books. Later she took to the prawn on which she killed many an autumn fish.

Major Huntington was no mean fisher himself. His best fish

from the Awe weighed 57 lb (July 1921; size 3/0 Mar Lodge), and the 51-pounder which he took from the same river in 1930 is possibly the largest hen fish caught in the UK. Grimble, too (*The Salmon Rivers of Scotland*) mentions the Huntingtons' 74 fish caught in 1912 on the Arndilly water of the Spey between 1st August and 15th October. No fish were caught during the First World War, and from 1920 the Huntingtons mainly fished on the Awe. Gladys Huntington was a tall, striking woman, rather formidable in appearance by all accounts but with a great sense of humour. She was essentially a countrywoman, a keen gardener and dog breeder and she loved the races. All of her five children became keen fishers at an early age.

THE WARDS

Lady Ward bought Kinnaird Estate with its fine 18th century house and 8,000 acres from the Duke of Atholl in 1926, but presumably the family had rented it for a few years before that as Kinnaird Fishing Book has records of Ward catches dating from 1922. And fascinating reading they make, interspersed as they are with newspaper clippings (referring not only to their own, but to other peoples' angling achievements) and photographs, giving a vivid picture of Society country life between the wars – croquet and tennis, stalking and shooting, picnics, but above all fishing. The Wards' main residence was at Chilton, Hungerford on the Kennet, where they had a splendid reach of water, but they generally fished in Scotland from August until October. From start to finish the Kinnaird fishing records provide extraordinary documentary evidence of consistent success both in numbers and in size of fish caught by the ladies of the family and their female friends. Lady Jean Ward, wife of Sir John, was the daughter of H. E. Whitelaw, American Ambassador in London, and she had inherited a large fortune from her mother. Considered the most expert of the country's Society lady anglers of the time, she was extremely keen and liked nothing better than wading all day in the river. She preferred to fish alone. On 10 October, 1927, Lady

Lady Ward in action at Kinnaird, River Tay.

Ward landed a 43 lb fish in Alderns, Upper Stobhall, and in Ferry Pool two years later she caught another 40-pounder. She fished at Kinnaird from 1922 until well into the 1950s and continued to land fish weighing more than 20 lb and several of over 30 lb.

On 13 September, 1955 at Dalguise, Lady Ward once more caught a 40 lb fish plus five others weighing 34, 16, 11, 13 and 21 lb (using Torrish fly and prawns).

Lady Mary Ward was another consistently successful fisher at Kinnaird, as was Lady Evelyn Ward, wife of the Hon. Gerald Ward, and both these ladies landed good numbers of substantial fish, often in series. A variety of flies were used by the Ward ladies, suggesting that they were probably randomly selected. Lady Mary for instance, took a 35-pounder on a Mar Lodge on 31 September, 1922 and the next day a 24-pounder on a Silver Grey. Wilkinson, Dusty Miller, Claret Jock, Jock Scott and Blue

Kinnaird House, now a fine hotel and restaurant.

Lettice Ward (left) with Esmé Glyn in the 1920s, and (right) anticipating a breakfast finnock.

Doctor all appear with regularity in the records and now and again the spoon crops up, or a golden sprat.

Miss Lettice Ward, bright young niece of Sir John and Lady Jean, makes her first appearance in the fishing book with a modest 17 lb salmon in September 1923, and the next year with two weighing 15 and 9 lb. She had to wait until 1927 (when she was 27), until she got a 25-pounder but one year later she surpassed all records at Kinnaird with a champion fish of 50 lb.

It was a lovely October day, says the fishing book, hot sun and with a slight wind from the east. Lettice chose a 'Kate' from the fly box and was fishing in Alderns where she hooked the monster and had a memorable struggle of fully $1\frac{1}{2}$ hours before the fish could be brought to gaff. As well as the 50-pounder she had already got two others weighing 19 and 12 lb. The big fish measured $51\frac{3}{4}" \times 27\frac{1}{2}"$.

On the same day Sir John fishing the Jetty Pool hooked a 44 pound fish and the story still circulates at Kinnaird of how he returned proudly to the house with his fine salmon (which he took on a prawn) to be completely nonplussed by young Lettice's monster. He did, none-the-less, have splendid casts made of the two, and these, along with casts of Lady Ward's 43 and 40 pound salmon, still adorn the billiard room at Kinnaird House which is now an exclusive country hotel and restaurant run by Mrs Ward, daughter-in-law of Sir John.

If 11 October, 1928 was Lettice's finest hour, she subsequently took a 37-pounder only four days later on Upper Stobhall and this at the end of a season which was considered unremarkable.

'The Tay,' reported the local newspaper, 'has experienced an indifferent season, both as regards rod and net fishing. Right from the commencement of the spring season there was a conspicuous shortage of small spring fish, followed by a similarly short crop of grilse ... '

Lettice's catches over the next couple of years were modest enough and in 1929 it was Lady Ward who got the 40-pounder with Lady Mary in second place with one of 32 lb, but in 1932, again in September (the 23rd) Lettice took a fish of 45 lb on a prawn, and next day which was very cold and squally with a south east wind and rain storms, having decided to try with a prawn again she caught a big fish of 37 lb.

Lettice married Anthony Wilson-Filmer in 1934, and her name appears with less regularity in the fishing book after that, but she did catch some respectable salmon at Kinnaird in later years.

There were frequent guests at Kinnaird and of the ladies who appear in the fishing book, several killed substantial salmon.

Lady Ward with a big fish and gillies at Kinnaird.

In 1927 Lady Wolverton caught a 32-pounder on a spoon at Lower Scone, and Esmé Glyn fishing Willie Stone took a 44-pounder. Indeed, of the four biggest fish landed from the Tay that season, three were taken by women. Apart from Esmé Glyn's achievement, Lady Ward had a 43-pounder and Miss Margaret Coats, who was fishing Sir Stuart Coats' water at Ballathie, landed a fine fish of 45 lb.

That was the year Miss Rachael Spender-Clay on the Spey at Fochabers landed a salmon which turned the scale at 36 lb beating Miss Isabel Beckwith's recent fine catch, though that was modest enough compared to Phillis Spender Clay's 47-pounder at the age of 13.

A record fish from the South. Mrs Shawe with the 48 lb salmon she took from the Hampshire Avon at Bisterne, April 1936.

MRS LECKIE-EWING

On Loch Lomond in the 1920s it was a lady again who completely altered the standard of values when it came to big fish, because for many years the capture of a salmon of 20 pounds had been a notable event there. Mrs Leckie-Ewing had moved to the lochside

The Leckie-Ewings at Loch Lomond. Her 36 lb fish from the loch caused a sensation in June 1927.

in 1922 with her husband, the major. They were both keen and experienced anglers and determined to make the most of the loch. So they made a careful study of the fishing grounds, thoroughly investigated local methods and tackle and equipped themselves accordingly. They learned to be in the right place at the right time, with the right equipment and were rewarded by a good many salmon and sea trout.

The Leckie-Ewings usually fished by themselves and on the afternoon of 30 June, 1927 they went out from Balmaha, the major rowing and his wife fishing. In no time at all a fish rose to the mallard and yellow dropper, head out of the water and jaws agape, and was firmly hooked – a big one. She fought it for an hour, the major well able to cope with the oars in a strong wave, before the salmon was successfully gaffed – a fine cock fish, in splendid condition. That evening they took it to Luss to be weighed and measured. It was 36½ lb in weight, 46 inches in length and 24 inches in girth and you can still see it today lying on the floor in Luss Public Hall in a progressively decaying condition, its glass case smashed, alongside the head of Mr Hamilton-Maxwell's record fish of 1886 – a mere 31½ lb.

PAMELA COLECLOUGH

Over the last 12 years Pamela Coleclough has caught a considerable number of salmon, and 10 of them have been 20 lb or over (three of 20 lb, two of 23 lb, one of 24 lb, two of 25 lb, one of 27½ lb, and one of 30 lb). They were all taken on fly, some sunk and some floating line, and all on the Delfur beat of the Spey in April and May. On the morning of 21 April, 1980 when she caught the 30-pounder she also took four others (7, 9, 10 and 11 lb).

'As a woman one feels, naturally, that it is a privilege to be allowed on the beat', says Mrs Coleclough. 'All hours are precious.' So she doesn't waste any time looking at the birds or scenery and fishes continually. Only a fly in the water will catch fish, she believes, and at the end of each cast she lets the fly come right round and always remembers what she was taught, that in fast running water it is best to leave the fly for quite a while when it has come round at the end of a cast, as this seems to be the time when most fish take.

Her most difficult large fish was taken in the middle of the Big Haddie pool. Almost as soon as she hooked it the spring in her fly reel broke, and she found it extremely hard to control the tension. She just had to let it run and she was taken from the neck to the tail of the pool and then through a lot of white water a fair way down-stream and through the neck and the tail of Island stream which was the next pool. Both she and the fish were exhausted at the end of the 90-minute battle but she certainly felt triumphant when she landed it. Usually she plays her fish hard. She thinks that the larger the fish the less active they become and that it's generally easier to land a large fish than a medium-sized one. As for hooking a large fish in the first place, Pamela Coleclough thinks it is entirely a matter of luck.

IVY HAYTON
(Whitby Esk record)

One fine September day in 1963 (the 28th) Ivy Hayton was having a picnic with her husband beside the Whitby Esk at Egton Bridge. Along came the river bailiff, so she asked his opinion as to the chances of getting a fish that day.

'If you care to fish the rough water and pools towards Glaisdale you might find a small sea trout,' said he, so after lunch the Haytons wandered up the river, and about 3.30 arrived at one of

Ivy Hayton with her record 30 lb salmon from the Whitby Esk.

the good holding pools, where Mr Hayton went to fish the run
in the pool and Ivy to try her luck at the bottom end. At about
4 pm the pool came to life with fish showing all over – and Mr
Hayton landed a good 7 lb sea trout. Just after that Ivy's line
suddenly went *zing*. She was certainly into a good fish! As soon
as it stopped running she retrieved the line furiously, then it set
off again. Her husband (an excellent gillie) was ready with the
gaff and soon had the fish on the bank. It was the biggest either
of them had seen come out of the Esk – a fine cock fish. Ivy was
thrilled, jumped up and down in delight admiring her fish, to be
told: 'Don't be so stupid, throw in and catch another!' This she

did, but unfortunately it got off. Ivy was sure that since the second
fish took her spinner from the same spot as the first one it must
have been female, as fish tend to pair up ready for spawning.
Ivy's fish was too heavy for their own scales so they called at the
bailiff's to have it weighed there.

'Would you like to see the small sea trout you said I might
catch?' said Ivy. He was amazed and thrilled at this fish, which
at $30\frac{1}{2}$ lb was the largest to come out of the Esk within living
memory. It remains the record for the Whitby Esk and Ivy's
ambition is to break it. She was by the way using a line with a
breaking strain of only 8 lb in those days and was told she'd
better get a stronger line. In 1966 she had another memorable
day – two salmon within an hour – $19\frac{1}{2}$ and 25 lb.

Ivy took up fishing because her husband fished. 'It makes for
harmony and a good relationship if a couple can pursue the same
hobby', she believes, 'and it usually has to be the *man's* choice
otherwise he will not play'. Male fishers, she feels, mostly like to
fish with their man friends, or alone. A lady is *lucky* to be invited
along. Now a widow, Ivy continues to fish the river which she
and her husband fished together for many years, 'with perhaps
even more determination than when he was alive.'

LADY JOAN JOICEY

Colonel Lord Joicey and Lady Joicey had rented the South Wark
beat of the Tweed (two rods) for the month of February 1935.
From the 4th to the 11th February they had 23 fish (Lord Joicey
five and his wife 18), on the 15th Lord Joicey caught seven and
Lady Joicey 28 (26 salmon and two sea trout) and in the rest of
the month the gentleman managed to catch 47 and the lady 55.
None of these fish exceeded 16 lb except one, which was caught
on the last day of the month by Lady Joicey, and which weighed

27 lb. There was great interest in Lady Joicey's catch of 28 fish at the time (a record for one rod on the Tweed) and how the fish were taken – all on a spinning bait:

> Upon the subject of salmon I am momentarily silenced, [read one report]. Returning from Ireland full of fishing stories, and those of salmon in particular, I find lying upon my desk a photograph of Lady Joan Joicey surrounded by a perfect holocaust of salmon. Offering her my heartiest congratulations I feel it impossible to try to emulate her feat, so shall retire to Sussex this weekend to fish for pike instead.

Lady Joicey, it is said, had two boatmen on that memorable day, one mounting golden sprats, and the other rowing all day with his bladder fit to burst, as he wasn't allowed ashore! In spite of the evidence though, Lady Joicey was not a fanatical fisher, – she was an excellent shot and passionate about horses and hunting – and if her catches consistently exceeded those of her husband this seems not to have disturbed their marital felicity!

LADY KIMBALL

The rivers of Scotland all have their 'idiosyncratic' rules, and there's a curious one on the Naver, which dates from 1919 when the river was sold by the Duke of Sutherland.

> ... under the rules of the River, each beat can only be fished by a maximum of 2 rods of which one must be a lady, or a boy under 18 years old. This has ensured that the river is not over-fished ...

Had the Duke waited another three or four years and assessed the record-breaking achievements of ladies in the early 1920s, he

Mary, 11th Duchess of Bedford (1865–1937) was well known for her pioneering flying exploits and is known as the 'Flying Duchess', but she was also a formidable fisher and on two occasions caught 13 salmon in one day angling on Stanley Water of the River Tay. She was a firm believer in the fly and used an 18-foot rod all day with the greatest of ease. She is seen in the photograph with the record catch of 2 April, 1913. The weights are: 22, 22, 19, 18, 17, 16½, 16, 15, 13, 10, 9, 7½, and 6½ lb. All were caught using the Black Dog, with the exception of one which fell to a Jock Scott. Other catches were, on 22 March, 23, 21, 21, 18, 14, 18, and 8½ lb; on 25 March, 15½ and 10½ lb; on 27 March, 23½, 19½, 18½, 18, 20, 20, 17½, and 14½ lb; on 5 April, 11, 18½, 14, 23, 10½, 10, 14, 9, 13, 14, 15, 16½, and 23 lb.

might well have considered banning them completely. But the rule stands to this day, ensuring equality and equal opportunity for those ladies lucky enough to be invited to fish there.

From 1945, most of the Naver fish were caught by the late Mrs Midwood, second wife of Ralph Midwood, and she was tutored by Jimmy Sutherland, the keeper at Syre. She became one of the best ladies on the river, but in 1956 Alec MacDonald, Head Keeper at Altnaharra, took on a new pupil in the shape of Lady Kimball, and she is considered by many to be the better of the two. Naver catches appear to be a closely-guarded secret – and I can only surmise that this is general policy, and guess at the reasons. Records of Lady Kimball's catches are therefore shrouded in mystery but Alec MacDonald recalls at least one 30-pounder. He also told me that Lady Kimball's mother-in-law was a formidable fisher too, and that she taught him a good deal about fishing when he was a young man.

LADY BURNETT

'Because of the ice on the English bank, we had to land the fish on the Scottish side of the river,' recalled Colin Swan who was working as boatman at Tilmouth Park Hotel on the Tweed in November, 1972. Lady Elizabeth Burnett was fishing the Pot Pool, and at about 11.30 am she hooked a large fish with a type of Garry tube fly. After playing it for 27 minutes Colin got it into the landing net. It was a cock fish of 43 lb, 47 inches in length and 27 inches in girth, and fresh run with sea lice.

'It was really just another day's fishing,' said Lady Burnett, 'just good luck!' But on that same morning she had taken another two, one of 17 lb and one of 10 lb! Lady Burnett doesn't regard herself as a fanatical fisher, although she is very keen. She enjoys doing lots of other things, too. Her first fishing was somewhere in the Alps, in Italy where she spent some years as a child, and later too as an adult. She has also fished in Canada.

Her 43-pounder won her the coveted Malloch Trophy for the biggest fish of the year from Scottish rivers. There was a wonderful party, at the Station Hotel, Perth, to celebrate, she recalls, and if there was any chagrin amongst the company that the Trophy had gone to the Tweed, there was no sign of it. Afterwards, in marvellous old-fashioned style, she stepped from the hotel dining-room straight onto the platform and into a southbound sleeper accompanied by the crate of fine malt which came with the trophy.

Lady Burnett's 43 lb Tweed salmon won her the Malloch trophy for the biggest fish of 1972 from Scottish waters.

The Pursuit of Excellence

⟡⟐⟡

'I have to say I have never seen a better all-round fly-fisher (male or female) with both single- and double-handed rods.'

Mr J. Cunningham of Newcastle upon Tyne, referring to Jean Green

JEAN GREEN

Jean Green's fishing is mostly (from choice) done on rivers, but she occasionally enjoys loch fishing for a change, especially 'with the prospect of contacting some very large sea trout'. As one of a minority of eccentric ladies who stand up to their waists in water all day, she is not sure if the word 'remarkable' applies to any of her achievements. She fishes fly only, and of the large number of salmon she has caught in many different rivers, the largest is $23\frac{1}{2}$ lb, which although very nice, is, she feels, nothing to write home about. Most of her fish are taken on single hooks.

There were a couple of occasions in her past experience when she *could* have made remarkable catches of salmon, but ceased fishing at such a prospect, as she had no desire to be a Bloody Butcher! Once she caught five salmon in virtually her first five casts, but recoiled at the thought of killing more so went home. It just happened, she thought, that conditions were perfect, and obviously there was a large shoal of fish ready to give themselves up. Regarding sea trout, although she has never given the matter much thought in terms of achievement, she does incidentally rather specialize in catching big ones, with the biggest at $13\frac{3}{4}$ lb, and over a period of years she has caught in excess of a hundred over 5 lb, many 7–10 lb with the odd 11- and 12-pounder. Significantly, they were all caught during the daytime and on a fly of course, mainly small singles. Many of these were caught on her local River Wear in Co. Durham. Certainly she considers the capture of each as a bit of an achievement because of their exceptional shyness and fighting abilities, and very often they have been caught under very difficult casting conditions. In fact she thinks this particular aspect of fishing to be one of the greatest challenges of all, and that the element of luck is very small. On the question of trout fishing, which Jean Green thinks also a very exacting form of fishing, apart from keeping the odd brace for the table, she returns virtually everything she catches – so is unlikely to break any records in this direction.

Jean Green on the Aberdeenshire Dee. A long cast from the left shoulder to counter upstream wind.

Jean Green: 'I do rather specialize in big sea trout.'

SHIRLEY DETERDING

Shirley Deterding is an artist and a formidably talented all-round sportswoman, a stalker, wildfowler, gameshooter, rider, scuba-diver, skier, motor-racer, foxhunter and yachtswoman. Her favourite pastime is fishing and she has travelled the world in pursuit of her quarry. A notably successful salmon fisher, she gives here an account of some memorable exploits:

> Half of successful fishing is sheer luck – being in the right place at the right time and meeting a 'taking' fish. Most of the very large fish caught and landed have been taken on spinning rods with lures but the satisfaction has always been hooking and landing a large fish on the fly rod – wherein lies far more skill.
>
> Most of the very large fish I have witnessed landed and caught myself have been on spinning tackle although other methods were thoroughly explored first – e.g. recently in Scotland a party fishing on Loch Arkaig for the reputed large Ferox, tried all day with different lures at different depths – then a small live-bait was used on a fly rod with a float and a large $12\frac{1}{2}$ lb Ferox was the result after a very exciting fight – another was lost shortly afterwards.
>
> One of my most memorable days fishing was in Norway on the River Vossö. I was in a party of men as a guest of Odd Haralson – being a mere female I was placed on the pools less renowned for producing fish and the gentlemen on the better pools. Each day I managed to produce a fish whereas they did not – the atmosphere got somewhat tense when on one particular day I managed three fish all around the 30 lb mark. One of the fish took me the whole length of the river, down the rapids into the fjord before it was finally landed on the banks – it was on this occasion,

having spun down the rapids, hitting rocks and in great danger of overturning, that concentrating hard on my fish I had not noticed the boat filling with water until the voice of Leidulv my gillie saying 'I hope you can swim' made me aware of the water creeping up to my knees. Playing the second fish later on in the day the line went round a large rock and the gillie took his clothes off and swam in the ice cold water to the rock and eased the line away to safety to land another fine big fish of 30 lb covered in sea-lice. The next fish was caught in the clear water of the lake above the river where no fish were ever hooked – much to my surprise we hooked a nice fish and after a tussle the gillie placed me on a rock in the middle of the lake to finally bring the fish to the gaff – as Leidulv skilfully put the gaff into the head of the fish, the gaff broke and the fish landed in the boat thrashing in a mess of line, blood and me who had slipped off the rock back into the boat – we all landed in the bottom of the boat together. That evening the gillie had taken the boat to the top of the pool to put it away for the night and I had a few casts off a groin at the end of the pool when my bait stopped – it came towards me and I saw the biggest fish of my life below me in the water – it must have weighed over 60 lb. It then suddenly realised it was hooked and took off downstream with me in hot pursuit and my line burning off my large Ambassador reel at such speed it 'smoked'. Yelling hard for the gillie I ran down the beat going through streams and bushes and rocks trying to check the fish – sadly and finally the line ran out and broke – my fish of a lifetime was no doubt in the fjord by now, several miles away trying to throw the bait.

Fishing is full of 'If only's', that's life! However – a day with three huge fish was a great triumph for me, especially as the men, as yet, were still fishless. I have a theory that

Shirley Deterding.

women are more sensitive and gentle in their approach to fishing and persevere more, or perhaps it's just Sixth Sense. I know I personally get a tingling sensation in my fingers seconds before I contact a fish.

On one occasion fishing the River Dee in the spring the river was rising fast and over the banks – it was Saturday night, in the dark. It was raining and cold and blustery, we had had no luck and then I saw a big fish move under a big iron bridge, a most difficult and long cast. On the third cast the fish took and the fun began. I could not move downstream as the flooded river in the dark had made progressing anywhere other than where I stood impossible. I had a struggle on my hands and time was against me too as the bewitching hour of midnight was fast approaching when fishing had to stop. After a lengthy and heart-stopping battle and several attempts to bring the fish to the net (it kept disappearing under the bank as the water was well above it by this stage) I eventually landed a beautiful fresh-run 25 lb fish – the biggest from that beat that season.

LESLEY CRAWFORD

Lesley is unusual amongst lady fishers in that she is married to a non-fisher. Her husband in fact is a 'Munro-bagger' in his spare time, and Lesley doesn't particularly enjoy struggling up mountains after him, so she concentrates on fishing which her father encouraged her to take up as a child.

She is a very keen angler and she also teaches fishing, and writes about it for the fishing journals. She fishes for trout and salmon in the wilds of Northern Scotland where she lives, and enjoys providing for her family. She would in fact argue that she possesses as much murderous intent as any male.

She believes that ladies are frequently more successful than men because 'while men tend to compete with one another while fishing, women compete single-mindedly with the fish. A man often becomes positively irate if the 'opposition' down the bank takes a bigger/better fish than he; and men generally view in terms of quantity of fish rather than the quality of the day as a whole. Even when alone a man competes with himself, to cast further, walk longer, land a fly in the most difficult spot and so on. Women

Lesley Crawford. 'Women compete single-mindedly with the fish.'

rarely get bogged down in this way, and enjoy all aspects of the outing, so catching fish ultimately becomes easier as they are more relaxed and they have a lighter touch.'

After considerable research among her lady angling colleagues Lesley has come across absolutely no support for any hormone/pheromone theory, and reaction to the idea had ranged from the indignant to the derisory. Today's female fishers, she says, are thinking anglers and conservationists, they excel at casting when properly taught and listen carefully to the gillie, while men often spurn advice considering it an affront to their fishing ability.

DIANA McANDREW

Diana McAndrew's reputation as a serious and formidable fisherwoman is far-reaching and stretches from the south of England to the north of Scotland. She wasn't born with a rod in her hand but married into a fishing family. Her parents-in-law used to rent a house and fishing on the River Broom in July and for two years Diana was happy enough just being a spectator or reading a book on the bank. Then, however, she decided she'd better learn to fish herself and so with a borrowed rod and some advice from her husband and father-in-law she started to teach herself. Her first fish was a $4\frac{1}{2}$ lb sea trout which she caught at around midnight in the Wall Pool, which is the first one up from the estuary. It happened to be the biggest sea trout on the river for some years but Diana was in any case feeling so pleased with herself that at 1 am she barged triumphantly into the bedroom of her sound-asleep father-in-law to show it to him. His enthusiasm was rather more muted than hers but after that she was considered capable of looking after herself. She was then sent to a pool further up the river where there was a chance of a salmon and in fact caught

Diana McAndrew with a 30 lb Spey salmon.

two that very morning, without any help and never having seen one landed before. This fired her enthusiasm for salmon fishing and she hasn't looked back.

She had an extraordinary fortnight on the Beauly in the autumn of 1988. The first morning she fished a big holding pool down twice with no success and her gillie Willie Matheson then told her it was 'now the time for shock tactics', and produced a very insignificant-looking $\frac{3}{4}$ inch orangy-brown 'home-tied' tube fly. Diana fished the pool again with some scepticism and soon hooked and landed a 25 lb cock salmon. She kept that fly on for a fortnight, it went up four trees, round a telegraph wire across the river, and was often under threat from her family who were after it. It caught 22 salmon (including the 25-pounder) out of a total bag of 49 with three other very able male rods fishing. It is called the 'Pull It' and Diana still guards it jealously. The first year Diana McAndrew came to live in Scotland she had a good many invitations to fish from friends here and there, often only for the day, and that year she managed to catch a fish on nine different Scottish rivers from the mighty Tay to the tiny Endrick water – all on a fly.

This is Diana's view of female success in salmon fishing:

> I do not believe that there is some sexual connection with the angling successes of females. I rather think that the female enthusiast is perhaps more capable of reading, thinking, and above all asking for and acting on any local advice available. Every river has its own totally different characteristic, and therefore to achieve success and catch a fish one's tactics must be infinitely adaptable.

MONSTER FISH FROM THE TAY

P. A. Oct. 10. 1942.

Beginner's Luck

❦

'I am not ... prepared to say that the history of the salmon stands free of all obscurity.'

Thomas Tod Stoddart, *The Angler's Companion to the Rivers and Lochs of Scotland*, 1853

ASHLEY SMITH

It was the October holidays and the last day of the fishing. My brother Michael had been fishing all week and had only caught a 10 lb salmon on Friday afternoon. I decided to give it a try as Michael had often said how easy it was. So mum, Michael, the gillie and myself decided to go fishing. It was getting near lunchtime and still no sign of a bite. I was just about to say we should go for lunch when my rod started jumping. I immediately picked it up and started to slowly wind in the line. There was a splash and I saw a quick glimpse of silver. I couldn't believe it. I had a salmon! The gillie soon told me that it was a hen fish as a cock fish was following.

After about five minutes I let my mum have a go at reeling it in as my arms were aching. It was getting closer to the boat and the gillie said that we should play it from the bank, so we landed on 'Mike's Bank' and played it from there. Everyone was really excited and after 15 minutes the fish was landed safely. The scales were quickly brought to weigh the fish. It weighed in at 24 lb. What a catch! Later on I was awarded a trophy for the largest fish taken on the Dalguise beat.

Ashley Smith caught her first fish, a 24 lb salmon, on the morning of Saturday 13 October, 1984, when she was eight. It was caught harling in the spot known as Mike's Bank above the Bridge pool on the Dalguise, River Tay. The boatman was Roy Arris, and it was the end of a very poor week when Ashley's only competition came from her six-year-old brother Michael.

Experienced male anglers had been fishing all Monday, Tuesday, Wednesday, Thursday, Friday and Saturday but had got nothing.

The bait was a 'Troutie' Kynoch Killer.

TRISH TIGHE

Sean Tighe had taken the Lees beat of the Tweed in the first week of September, 1988. The weather was atrocious and by day three, he wasn't doing well at all. His wife Trish had been sick all night and was feeling miserable. She wasn't a keen fisher either, and in one year of marriage had tried only a few flicks of a fly rod. Sean thought the prospects were hopeless enough to let Trish fish and that some fresh air would be good for her, so he got her into the boat, set her in the swivel seat while he sat in the bow to offer his pearls of wisdom, and the gillie rowed in the middle.

After about five minutes the 20g Silver Toby was slung about 40 yards, but slightly upstream. This was considered good enough to fish round for the first time. Trish was gently winding as instructed, and half way round she said 'Ooh ... something touched it!' Her sceptical husband replied that it was probably flotsam, but had not told her what to do if a fish *did* take, thinking this extremely unlikely. He was much more concerned about

Jean Green in action. Excellent form in overhead casting results in a long smooth shoot. On the Tees at Hurworth (below) she stays out of the water and casts up to 30 yards to avoid scaring large shy fish. (See page 67.)

Ashley Smith with her 24 lb Tay salmon (see page 79).

getting her to throw the lure in a semblance of the correct distance and direction.

Half way round the next cast though, he was surprised to see the rod tip making very fish-like movements. Various unprintable expletives followed and a heated dialogue during which Trish's husband tried to get the rod from her. No hope of that however. Trish was by now as hopelessly hooked as her fish, and determined to follow it through.

And so she did. The gillie netted a fine fish, weighing 18 pounds and covered in sea-lice. But that isn't the end of the story. Five minutes and three casts later Trish was into another fish which was landed without incident and weighed 7 pounds. Sean Tighe took over then and fished the pool thoroughly for another hour and a half without a touch, then for the next two days. He caught nothing and left the Tweed in a thoughtful mood.

Trish Tighe. A fine brace from the Tweed in 'hopeless' conditions.

PRETTY DRY

Young Beginner (fishing with dry fly). " Am I keeping my fly properly dry, Duncan ? "

Scots Keeper. " Oh, I'm thenkin' she'll be dry enough. She's stickin up in that big willow near by where ye started fushin'."

A McCorquodale showing early prowess. Seven-year-old Sophie van Cutsem, daughter of Geoffrey and Sally (née McCorquodale) van Cutsem, with a 10-pounder from the Helmsdale, 1983. With this catch she became the first child of the fifth generation of Harold McCorquodale to take a fish from the river.

Janet Popham. 'Janet got a 22-pounder on No. 1 beat on Upper Stables Pool on a Jock Scott.' This was the terse entry in Hugh Popham's diary for 1 April, 1908 and he didn't think it worth recording that this was his new bride's first ever fish and only her second day's fishing. A brilliant start to the honeymoon? A wooden model of the fish adorned the family home for many years.

ANABELLE HAWTREY

Annabelle Hawtrey.

On 22 May, 1951 Anabelle Hawtrey was fishing with her father and grandfather on the River Garry at Killiecrankie. She had been fishing dry fly for trout and was getting bored as the men had been catching salmon. So she asked if she could have a try and was later found a light salmon rod, an old reel with a brake that didn't work, last year's line with a knot in it and her own prawn tackle. She went down to the river next morning to the Soldier's Leap. The water was a bit fast so she clambered up a rock to get round the point where it runs into the viaduct pool. She cast across to the far side – but not far enough, so she fished it out, cast again and got stuck. Or so she thought. She heaved on the rod with no effect, then her rod tip bounced and very slowly the line moved across the pool. She realised it was a fish and that she must try to get it to a landing place. The fish kept to the bottom so she couldn't move him, but eventually she managed to get the line over some high rocks and round a tree. The fish tore down the pool, the line shot out and so did the knot that she knew was the weak spot. Then he came back again and went upstream and round a submerged rock, where she could see the line chafing.

Anabelle's father arrived and looked on (he thought the salmon was about 16 lb) and they both saw the fish leap out of the water on the lip of the pool before the run to the next pool. With a lot of heaving the fish came back up and she played it for another 20 minutes before they eventually gaffed it. The fight had lasted for an hour and 20 minutes. The salmon was 44 inches long and weighed just on 30 lb on the Killiecrankie railway station scales. Anabelle was just 15 years old and it was her second salmon.

BARBARA CARTLAND

Barbara Cartland, who in the 1989 *Guinness Book of Records* was listed as the world's best-selling author with over 500 million books sold, married a McCorquodale, or rather she married two, first of all (in 1927) Alexander, formerly of the Argyll and Sutherland Highlanders. So naturally she was soon introduced to the family beat on the Helmsdale. Barbara had been to Scotland several times before (in fact the Cartlands have Lanarkshire connections dating back to the 11th century) but until 1927 she had not been so far north. She was entranced by the beauty of the Strath and when she was taken out fishing the day after she arrived she caught her first salmon. It weighed 14 lb and she also

Barbara Cartland with menfolk and dogs on the Helmsdale.

caught three others on the same day. She had never fished before. Over the years she became a really proficient salmon fisher and caught several hundreds, but that first has a place of honour in the Heritage in Helmsdale where there is a Barbara Cartland room.

Her marriage to Alexander was dissolved in 1933, but her second husband Hugh was also a McCorquodale and her three children are all McCorquodales, and so the traditions continue. And at 89 Barbara's heart is still in the Highlands although it is many years since she has caught a fish.

On one occasion on the Helmsdale when the weather was rather too sunny and the water much too low Barbara was teasing the men of her party for not managing to catch any fish. 'I'd like to see you doing any better,' said one exasperated angler. So of course next morning the lady repaired to the river and after a few casts hooked a salmon, landed it shortly afterwards and brought it back to the lodge in triumph.

JENNY BIDWELL

Lady Bidwell was introduced to fishing by her husband as he thought she was becoming bored watching. 'She's certainly better than I am now,' says Sir Hugh, who is Lord Mayor of London. But he didn't teach her to cast and wisely left that to gillies: 'Teaching your wife to cast is like teaching your wife to drive, best left to someone else!'

Lady Bidwell caught her first salmon in 1989 and 'There was no question of the excitement, particularly as I was not expecting to be fishing myself.' They were on the river Naver, at Upper Cearn-na-coille, and had, she remembers, unexpectedly $1\frac{1}{2}$ rods to be used for either a man and a lady or a man and a boy (under 18).

'We were with family and friends, Sir James and Lady Clemenson, in fact it was on Lady Clemenson's rod and with her fly, a Monroe Killer, that I caught my first fish. Then on our next day I caught two further fish ...' Sir Hugh was delighted when she caught her first salmon although by the second day when she caught her third, she thinks he might have become just a little envious as he hadn't had a touch.

Jenny Bidwell's life normally revolves around State and other formal functions in the capital, so it is perhaps not surprising that she has a passion for the countryside and nature; and fishing, she finds, best complements her life in the City.

Lady Bidwell thinks that female angling success is all down to luck. Although perhaps it's because women are often more patient.

MISS STEWART

Miss Stewart and her mother were members of a party at Fasnakyle in Lower Affric in the 1930s. Mrs Stewart was an experienced fisher but her daughter had never fished before. At the Lodge there was a daily programme where some of the party would go off stalking and others would fish the river. One day several fishers were allocated pools, and there was a lot of teasing and banter as to who would catch the biggest fish. Duncan MacLennan was the gillie assigned to Mrs and Miss Stewart, and the previous day he had shown the young lady how to cast on the lawn using a salmon rod and line, but no hook. He put down a marker and made her practise casting until she could place the top of the line beside it. When her arm tired Duncan would sit down with her under a tree and explain how she should strike, with an upward movement of the rod-point when a fish rose, and how to handle rod and reel when playing a fish. He explained the various flies and recounted his own experiences of catching and losing fish. They spent the entire afternoon in this manner and Duncan said that Miss Stewart was very interested in all he had to say, and very patient.

When, next day, he took the two ladies to the Island Pool, a broad, shallow, fast-flowing pool, he got Mrs Stewart to start halfway down the pool so as to keep the easier stretch for her daughter. Miss Stewart sat with Duncan on a bench by the pool and he pointed out how skilfully her mother was covering it. Then with an encouraging pat on the shoulder he told her to start, and to keep an eye on her fly. After a few casts the rod point bent and the reel skirled as the line ran out burning her fingers. 'I've got one, Duncan,' she shouted and he was fast by her side telling her to keep the rod point up, and when to reel in and let out line. After an hour and fifteen minutes, with an excited Mrs Stewart witnessing the battle, Duncan was able to net a splendid 22 lb salmon, the biggest ever to come from that river to his knowledge.

They had the prize for the day, but also for many a day to come. People put it down to beginner's luck but Duncan MacLennan reckons it was simply good fishing by someone who patiently listened to advice and went about her fishing in a sporting and skilful manner.

Great Expectations

༺☾ཊঌ☽༻

'Angling for salmon, in any shape, is a noble sport.'

Delabere P. Blaine, *An Encyclopaedia of Rural Sports*, 1858

FIONA WILLIS

Fiona Willis was eight months pregnant when she arrived with her husband James for a week's fishing on the Dounie beat of the River Carron in Sutherland and a few eyebrows were raised. The first two days were blank, but on the Wednesday morning James caught a fish on the lower part of the beat. After lunch Fiona opted for the Captain's Pool as it could be easily fished without wading, and James headed off up river to try the very top pools. It was agreed that if Fiona needed him urgently (if she caught a fish for instance, if she fell in, or she went into labour) she would whistle.

She selected a 3″ black and yellow Waddington from her fly box and started to fish. When she was about two thirds of the way down the pool her line tightened, gently at first. She lifted her rod and prepared to play what she assumed to be a typical 8 or 9 pound Carron fish which she would be happy to land alone. But the fish started to take line like nothing she had ever seen before and things changed dramatically. As she battled to keep her rod tip up, she desperately tried to whistle and managed twice before she had to divert all her attention to recovering her line. The fish came back up to almost the point where it was hooked and she whistled again. A few moments later James appeared, and they both caught a glimpse of the fish's tail, a long way from the drowned line. The shallows obviously upset him and he headed off again right down the river and towards the small torrent at the top of Mrs Ross; he took all the line and started on the backing before stopping, and at this point Fiona decided that she didn't want to join him for a swim, and so she started to fight as hard as he was fighting. She had him about half way back up when she got cramp in her arm and was very grateful to hand over the rod for a few minutes' break.

After just over an hour they attempted to net him but got nowhere near as he decided to head upstream for a change. As they brought him back in he swam very close to a small croy and Fiona's heart sank as she envisaged the line snagging and breaking, and her beautiful fish disappearing.

James took the rod and went to the end of the croy, leant out as far as he could and persuaded the fish away after a few more hair-raising moments. After a total of one hour and 10 minutes they managed to land him high on the bank. Fiona was exhausted.

Later that evening the gillie called to see how they had done and was amazed when they showed him the fish. They hadn't had any scales to weigh it, so he did, and proclaimed it a glorious 25-pounder. He then disappeared with it and it's understood that Fiona's fish visited a considerable number of people that evening. It was years later that the gillie admitted to Fiona how horrified he had been when she had announced that she was planning on fishing 'in that state' and that her husband was letting her!

Both sets of parents were telephoned that night and early next morning James phoned his sister with the news. When she told her half-asleep husband he muttered that his wife must have got the figure wrong – 'Babies don't come that big'. The Willises' daughter was born a month and three days later, and she weighed 7lb 6oz.

PATRICIA WOTHERSPOON

Patricia Wotherspoon doesn't consider herself a real killer, and still, after many years of fishing, has some reservations about it. She took up the sport in her courting days and of course by marrying Alistair, the second son of Inverness's Provost Robert Wotherspoon, she was assured immediate access to wonderful fishing and stalking territory – the Wotherspoons owned Glen Affric Lodge and also had the fishing on the Ness. Patricia and her family lived for many years well within earshot of the river and gillie Lindesay Wood often stopped by for coffee and chat at Patricia's house Benula.

One beautiful warm, sunny day in June 1955, Patricia was in that final stage of pregnancy, with plans laid and preparations complete, full of energy and anticipation – but a trifle bored, and looking forward to seeing her feet again. Lindesay had a free day so suggested that the two of them go for a quiet cast. A great character, Lindesay was well in his seventies at the time but gallant as always – and only mildly apprehensive about loading the boat with this rather ungainly lady. They walked upstream to the boat, planning a leisurely fish in the Black Stream which lay almost directly opposite the house and so within hailing distance in case some domestic crisis should arise. Patricia cast away contentedly with Lindesay's favourite Hairy Mary when suddenly her fly was taken by a heavy fish which dashed away at full speed, tearing out line with that exciting sound of the screeching reel, then going down deep, a dead weight so still that she began to wonder if she'd hooked a rock after all. Full of anxiety, Lindesay tried to persuade her to hand him the rod, but Patricia indignantly refused. The fish sulked. Silence ... Waiting ... Trying to keep the right tension on the line to be aware of his mood, then off again with tremendous strength and fantastic noise of the reel. A gentle attempt to persuade him to come nearer and his renewed panic as he became aware of the boat and his impending fate. Patricia found herself scrambling round the boat (to Lindesay's horror) to keep the fish from going underneath, and finally, almost sadly, he was persuaded to glide benignly in towards the bank and Lindesay's waiting net. He was a great dark cock fish with an ugly kype and weighed $26\frac{1}{2}$ lb when suspended with difficulty in the same spring balance that had been used to weigh Patricia's first daughter, and the excitement helped to persuade Patricia's overdue second daughter to join their rather crazy household a few days later!

DAVINA MORLEY

Davina Morley and her husband were invited by American friends to fish the Vossö in Norway in June 1987. It is a big, swift river running through a deep and narrow rocky valley, with plenty of white water, and it is mostly fished by boat. The Bolstad beat is roughly $1\frac{1}{2}$ miles long running out into the head of the fjord. The sea-bound fish don't normally return for three or four years, so they tend to run big.

Davina was accompanied for the evening session on June 7th by a young, but experienced English gillie. The Norwegian gillies had politely declined to accompany her since she was eight months pregnant, and frequently you have to 'shoot the rapids' if the fish takes you downstream making for the fjord.

After fishing the Bridge Pool they made their way downstream, the river bank so covered with wild flowers it was hard to know where to tread. Charlie suggested having a cast in a peculiar-looking backwater, common to all strong-flowing rivers. The river was very fast white water just beyond and Charlie told her to cast into that, let the line come towards her and wait. A fish took and hurtled straight out into the white water where Davina

Davina Morley with her splendid Vossö salmon, 40 lb.

played him for a bit, then he played dead and sulked using his power and a strong-flowing current. Charlie rushed off for the net, then the fish jumped and she saw that he was big! There's an extraordinary bush telegraph on this river and if someone is into a big fish, the fisherman is not alone for long. Lots of help and advice was soon forthcoming and, when they decided to take the fish downstream there were offers to take the rod, especially when she had to climb a post and rail fence. Davina however, was determined not to give in despite her huge and inconvenient tummy and the fish was landed after 40 minutes – a splendid cock fish of 40 lb. When at last she saw him on the bank, 'his huge depth and glistening paleness', she was rather sad – he seemed too magnificent to die.

After short celebrations and weigh-in, Davina returned to the Bridge Pool and very soon caught another beautiful fish of 20 lb. Any fish of 20 lb and under is automatically given to the local river owners but Davina has her large fish mounted (by Allan Allison of Kinross) in a glass case in her hall – a permanent reminder of that wonderful evening. The Morleys' third son Henry was born a month later.

Davina took up fishing when she married a keen fisherman, but it was something she had always wanted to do – she *knew* she would love it. The trouble with salmon fishing, she told me, is that it's so expensive, and she found that as a single girl the invitations were not forthcoming. 'You weren't asked if you couldn't fish, so how could you learn?'

Pioneers at Home & Abroad

*'You are a strange combination, Jean,' remarked her cousin.
'You fish, shoot, and hunt, wear short skirts and knickerbockers,
and yet you are the tenderest hearted thing in the world.'*

Ethel B. Tweedie, *Wilton, Q.C., or, Life in a Highland Shooting Box*, 1895

MRS E. S. TAIT

In October 1932 a Canadian lady set a world record by catching
a 43 lb Pacific Coast salmon on a trout rod and fly. Mrs Tait was
fishing off Vancouver Island, BC, for cohoes, the smaller of the
two varieties of Pacific salmon which can be taken on rod and
line. She had already caught several fish and as she cast again, a
big fish took and ran.

> How he ran! He took my line right out to the last couple
> of turns on the reel, and then, for some reason, stopped,
> and saved me from losing all my line, and, incidentally,
> from heart failure!

A ding-dong struggle ensued, the angler winning back some on
her reel, only to have it stripped off again as the salmon made
another rush time after time. At last Mrs Tait succeeded in getting
the tiring fish near the boat, and was dismayed and thrilled as
she glimpsed its broad back to realize that she was attached to a

Mrs E. S. Tait. A 43-pounder on light tackle, October 1932.

huge spring salmon instead of a big cohoe, as she had thought. With no gaff in the boat they were in a predicament, but fortunately a boy in a canoe came along and assisted in gaffing the fish. No sooner did the fish touch the bottom of the boat than out fell the hook. Mrs Tait was certainly in luck that day, for the splice joining her line to the backing was badly frayed, and would not pass through the top ring without hitching up but, as she gaily remarked, 'little annoyances like that only added to the fun of the fight.'

The tackle used by Mrs Tait is worth noting ... Her rod was a Hardy 'Houghton' 10 ft. The reel was a $3\frac{5}{8}$ in. Hardy 'Perfect', with 70 yards of line and backing; a Campbell river Bucktail fly, No. 1/0 hook, and a 'Red Loop' quarter-drawn cast completed the outfit. Perhaps it will take an angler to appreciate to the full Mrs Tait's achievement in landing a 43 lb salmon on such light tackle, but it was undoubtedly a notable feat.

THE ICELANDIC MAIDENS

'Of these islands it must be confessed, that they have not many allurements, but to the mere lover of naked nature,' wrote Dr Johnson of the Scottish Islands in 1775. One shudders to think what he'd have had to say about Iceland, a thousand miles or so further north, virtually treeless and infinitely more bleak and barren. Having a low opinion of angling too, the doctor would not even have been attracted by any of Iceland's 64 salmon rivers. Twenty of these are considered first-class and so unspoiled Iceland, in an increasingly polluted world, is offering considerable charms to the adventurous (and affluent) fly fisher. The island is surprisingly large, nearly twice the size of Scotland, much larger than Ireland, yet with a population of only 250,000, mostly concentrated around Reykjavik on the south-west coast. The interior is practically uninhabited. The best fishing areas are on the west and north coast, and Iceland excels not so much in size of fish, but in numbers, because netting is less widely practised there. Usually, a two sea-winter fish averages 8–12 lb, a three sea-winter fish 16–25 lb and on the Laxa i Adaldal river ('Laxa' simply means salmon river) there's at least the remote chance of hooking a 20-pounder.

In Iceland, as elsewhere, the ladies are having more than their fair share of the fish, and they are getting the big ones, too. Icelandic women are independent and liberated by any standards, but until very recently there was an even smaller percentage of women fishing there than in the UK for example. In the 1920s there was one pioneering lady who was an avid fisher, but she was exceptional, and if things are changing now and women are beginning to interest themselves in their husbands' sport it is largely due to the example of Gudrún Bergmann. Gudrún is a dynamic career woman, a mother, a superb fisherwoman, and she has also written a comprehensive guide to Icelandic fishing for the Angling Club of Reykjavik. In 1989, Gudrún noted there were quite a few large salmon caught in the river Hrutafjardara in the north of Iceland. All of them were caught by women, some of whom were catching their first-ever salmon.

On 4 July Alfa Hjàlmarsdóttir caught a $19\frac{1}{2}$ lb salmon in Mariubakki pool. The pool is a long one in the lowest part of the river and fly, worm and spoon are permitted. Alfa's husband and their friend were fishing together, and her husband started off, working the pool about five times, each with a different fly. Then came the friend's turn with the worm and finally Alfa with the spoon. She caught three salmon, the biggest one $19\frac{1}{2}$ lb, while the men looked on.

At the beginning of September Edda Vikar Gudmundsdóttir was fishing with her husband in Hrutafjardara. Just below Réttar-foss there is a long pool called Réttarstrengur and her husband started fishing it with the fly. He went over it a few times using different flies with no success, so told her it was now her turn. She went out with the worm and threw the bait in at the top of the rapids. A fish took immediately and after a great fight lasting about 30 minutes, (during which time her reel failed) she landed a salmon of 18 lb.

Also in September, Hronn Albertsdóttir was fishing in Hruta-fjardara with her husband; neither of them had ever caught a salmon before although they had fished for trout. They went up a side river called Sika to the top pool called Sikarfoss. As was the usual pattern, the husband started off fishing with the fly, and went over the pool several times using different ones. Since he was having no luck, he told her she could have a try. Hronn walked out to a cliff (under which the fish are supposed to lie), threw the worm in and immediately hooked one. It dived deep and went under the cliff she was standing on, then went to the bottom of the pool and up again a few times. At one point the line went slack and she thought she had lost him, but she found on reeling in that he was still there. They had a hard time beaching it and because she was so inexperienced she didn't realise that she ought to have left the cliff and gone a little further down the river to find an easier spot. Finally they made it, and triumphantly brought back a 22 lb salmon. Being her first, it was a great catch.

THURIDUR INGIMUNDARDOTTIR

Thuridur's husband works as area manager at Svarta for the Angling Club of Reykjavik, and for several years her family had opened the season there. While Thuridur had been on lots of fishing trips she was usually happy to participate vicariously through her husband and children. But she had taken the rod occasionally and had caught a few small trout.

On 1 July, 1984 Thuridur's family was fishing on the lower part of the river. Her 15-year-old son caught two salmon, then her 10-year-old daughter caught one, but her husband only hooked and lost one. Thuridur then decided to try for 'the big one', so she put on a few worms and cast into a pool where the Svarta and Blanda meet – fresh water and muddy glacier water. She hardly saw the salmon take, but the line pulled upstream and she followed. When the fish had raced to the top of the pool it stopped and sulked. All of a sudden it turned and dashed downstream. Then another powerful rush upstream followed and again the fish returned and sulked. Thuridur was beginning to doubt whether she was in control and was meanwhile being bombarded with technical advice from the experts. But after a while the fish surfaced and they could see that he was a big one and she very nearly lost heart and almost handed the rod to her husband. The salmon made two fabulous leaps, then a third and her heart missed a beat! Then it darted down below the bend and headed for the main current in the river Blanda on the other side of an island. That might very well have been the end because she couldn't have followed it, but fortunately it turned back into the stream nearer to her and headed down. By this time it was tiring and Thuridur was feeling more confident and she was able to beach it shortly afterwards. The drama lasted about half an hour and this fish, her first salmon, weighed $18\frac{1}{2}$ lb.

Thuridur's husband Grettir Gunnlaugsson by the way has fished since childhood in rivers all over the country, he has worked a lot for the Angling Club of Reykjavik and is now chairman of the National Association of Angling Clubs in Iceland but has not managed to date to catch a fish as big as his wife's.

KRISTIN STEINGRIMSDOTTIR

It was a beautiful evening in August 1984, the sort of weather where you don't catch much in 'Ida', but Kristin decided to try her luck after dinner. She took a casting rod, as there are steep cliffs and it isn't easy to use a fly rod. She tied on a double hook Butcher no. 4 and some sinkers and waded into the river. After two or three casts she was into a fish, a big one which tore line from her reel. She didn't give him much room, reeled in and when he came closer he turned in the water and she saw just how big he was. After a fight of 20 or 30 minutes she had him beached. As she knocked the fish on the head, the fly fell out so she felt she must have come pretty close to losing him. Kristin struggled home with her salmon to show it to her husband and to have it weighed – a big fish for Iceland, 24 lb.

GUDRUN OLAFSDOTTIR

Gudrún was fishing in late July, 1976 in the Vidialsa river in north Iceland in Dalsaros pool. She hooked a salmon on a Toby spinner and found it so heavy to reel in that she finally decided to lock the reel and just walk backwards. So she didn't actually see how big the fish was as it came out of the water, but only heard the screams and shouts of her fishing friends. It weighed 25 lb.

JONA VIGFUSDOTTIR

One beautiful autumn evening in late August 1988, Jóna Vig-fúsdóttir was fishing in the Svarta river in northern Iceland. They were fishing upriver and had decided to try a promising pool named Hrossabeinahvammur (Horse-bone pool). They went down quietly to the river and Jóna's husband anxiously scanned the pool. It was lit by the rays of the late sun and he saw three salmon lying lazily quite close in. Two of them were a respectable size and one was truly a huge brute. Jóna's husband was tremendously excited she recalled, and naturally because of his 'enormous experience' decided to try first, so she sat down to watch, a short distance from the pool. He put a few worms on the hook and cast out. (When he is telling tall fishing stories to his friends, says Jóna, her husband only mentions flies!) In any case nothing happened and after 10 or 15 minutes he gave up and handed the rod to Jóna. After her second cast she heard her husband yell and she was very surprised as he's usually very quiet when fishing. But she soon understood what he was excited about when she felt as if a giant was pulling her rod. A few moments later a huge salmon leapt from the water and then began a fierce fight. It was by far the largest fish Jóna had ever encountered and she was nervous to say the least. Her husband came to help her but it soon became apparent that he was too excited to be of any use, giving all kinds of conflicting commands ... up with the rod ... down with the rod ... don't let it get upstream ... let it get upstream, etc.

'I simply quit listening to him,' said Jóna, 'and did it like Frank Sinatra, that is, my way. After some time (it felt like ages, but was probably no more than half an hour), I managed to steer the fish into shallow water. There it had to give up its gallant fight, but before it decided to call it quits, it did a triple somersault much like Mary Lou Retton in the 1984 Olympics, and it snapped the rod cleanly in two pieces. Then I realized that perhaps my husband wasn't so bad after all, because he plunged into the river and managed to seize the fish with both hands and heave it ashore. It weighed about 19 lb – not bad for a little lady.'

GUDRUN (GUNNA) BERGMANN

The river Laxa a Asum is in the north of Iceland and although it is quite a small river it has more salmon than most, and it is quite normal for someone to catch up to 20 salmon a day, which used to be the limit. After the limit was abolished Gunna and her husband Gulli caught 50 salmon in one day in the Laxa river between 8.00 am and twelve noon.

On 14 August, 1986 Gunna and Gulli were fishing this river from pool to pool, and while one fished the other went ahead to the next one. Gunna had gone ahead of Gulli and as she saw him coming towards her she started casting. When the fly (a red Black-Eyed prawn fly, tied by Peter Deane) hit the water the second time, a salmon grabbed it. Gunna hardly had time to realise one was on when it started jumping like crazy in the pool, and when she saw how big it was she shouted and Gulli came running, not believing what she had said about having 'the big one' on this time. It seemed as though the salmon had, while still jumping, rolled the line around itself and when it came down to calmer water and they were able to see it, Gulli alarmed her by saying that she had probably foul-hooked it. Luckily Gulli was wrong, though the salmon played oddly (the line was twisted round the gills) so it took less time to subdue than normal for a fish this size, and the fight was not hard. After about 45 minutes they were able to beach him and Gulli took him by the tail and carried him five or six metres away from the river. Gunna's triumphant cry could be heard for miles around and when Gulli was about to unhook the fly without first stunning the salmon with the priest, she flatly refused on the grounds that he might get away. The salmon weighed 24 pounds, the biggest Gunna had ever caught, and also the biggest from the Laxa a Asum river.

MAXINE EGAN

Maxine Egan started her fishing in the trout streams of Oregon at the tender age of seven, and she has been fishing ever since

Maxine Egan, big fish specialist from the steelhead country.

(over half a century). She took up steelhead fishing while living beside the Seymour River near Vancouver, BC, at a time when it was rare to see a woman fishing for steelhead, particularly during the cold, often wet and windy winter season when the best runs take place. Maxine probably would have attracted the attention of Vancouver sports writers just because she *was* a woman, and a very attractive one at that, but her skills at fishing for steelhead were as good if not better than many of the male steelheaders, and during the 1950s and '60s her exploits were often the subject of West Coast Canadian sports writers.

Maxine is the only woman twice to win the Lillian Sparrow Trophy of the Tyee Club of British Columbia (a trophy for the largest tyee salmon caught by a woman each year). She did it in August 1964 with a tyee of $47\frac{1}{2}$ lb and again in the summer of 1989 with one of 48 lb.

Maxine's largest fish was an estimated 55 lb tyee salmon that she caught in the Campbell River (Vancouver Island) in 1955, and released after a fight of nearly two hours. Like her husband Van Egan, she is a good all-round angler, fishing flies for trout and steelhead.

CLARE DE BURGH

By the light of the midnight sun at 3 am on 9 July, 1968 on the Alta river, Norway, Clare de Burgh hooked a large salmon. She was using a 12 foot split cane rod and the same yellow bucktail tube fly which she had used regularly on the river Slaney in Ireland. Mrs de Burgh, who is considered by many to be Ireland's best fisher, thought herself very lucky, first of all to be invited to fish the Alta by her American host Seward Johnston, and then to be in the right place at the right time! In fact she always reckons that luck plays the most important part in fishing.

The pool in which she hooked this big one was Svartfossnakken Pool just above the Svartfoss rapids, where boats have to be hauled overland, and the adventure which followed was the most hair-raising of her entire fishing career. Problems arise at Svartfoss if a hooked fish chooses to descend the rapids, and that's exactly what Clare's fish did on this occasion. Very few gillies would have been prepared to follow it, but the two young Norwegians with Clare de Burgh were fearless and strong. They told her to lie down in the boat, while with the outboard motor flat out, they pulled as hard as they could against the current and made a rough descent. A truly terrifying experience, and the feat had in fact only been accomplished once before within living memory. It was $2\frac{3}{4}$ hours after the first sighting before the fish was seen again and an attempt made to gaff it. This was unsuccessful and the gaff broke, but fortunately help had arrived at the scene (when a big fish is hooked the word spreads fast by bush telegraph) and a larger gaff was brought. The monster was finally landed $4\frac{1}{2}$ miles down stream from where it had been hooked. It was too heavy for the lodge scales but it was taken to the next lodge downstream where the Duke of Roxburghe was staying and a weight of 53 lb was recorded. It was a cock fish, 52 inches long and 29 inches in girth.

Clare de Burgh has fished in Scotland, Iceland and Canada besides Ireland and Norway but thinks that her first visit to the Alta was her most exciting-ever fishing:

> I had a wonderful week killing 25 salmon averaging 24 lb, largest 33 lb, as well as three grilse. On my last night (we start fishing at 8 pm until 4 am) I caught seven salmon and one grilse and played and lost two more salmon.

They had to stop at 3 am as they were leaving for home that morning and Clare later wrote in her fishing book: 'The best and luckiest salmon fishing that I have ever had.' There were six rods

Clare de Burgh in Norway. Down the rapids with a 50-pounder.

and the total was 78 fish for the week. The next year, when she caught the 53-pounder, there were few fish in the river due to the late spring, and it was very hard work for the seven rods to make a total of 35 fish, of which Mrs de Burgh caught seven averaging 27 lb. The great joy about that river, she recalled, was that it was 'fly only'.

Mrs de Burgh loved her visits to Iceland, too; all three rivers were very different, and her favourite was the Nordura where she caught 29 fish in six days, the largest 18 lb. Other notable days were 10 fish (April 1980) from the Upper Kinnaird Castle beat on the S. Esk, (six fly and four bait) and at Careysville, two unforgettable June days in 1984 when she took 17 fish all on Esmund Drury tied flies.

Luck apart, Clare de Burgh feels that any success she has had is probably due to the fact that from the age of seven she was brought up to fish dry fly for trout on a chalk river in Gloucestershire, and this taught her to be accurate, delicate and to keep out of sight as much as possible.

MARY JANE RYMPA

Mary Jane Rympa fishes each year in June near Førde in Norway, and in 1984 she was *particularly* 'lucky'.

Mary Jane Rympa with the 46-pounder from Førde, Norway.

She was fishing from the boat, when she had a strange feeling that something was out there. She could feel that one was lurking! After casting for some time the gillie suggested changing the shrimp. It took about ten casts before her intuition was proved. It was a big one – 46 lb – the largest salmon caught there in the last 30 years, and the event was reported in the local newspaper.

Mary Jane, who lives in Leamington Spa, was brought up in Minnesota by the Mississippi in a family where fishing was an accepted tradition for both boys and girls. 'Pan-fishing' was how she started, and the eating was important! She simply cannot understand 'coarse-fishing' practice in Britain, where fish are returned to the water after a period of torture. In the States she fished for perch, bass, sun-fish, pike and so on and found ice-fishing great fun. It wasn't, all the same, common or accepted back home for girls to fish, and most would have been reluctant to bait the hooks with live worms.

LADY MALLABAR

Lady Mallabar married twice, and both husbands were keen fishermen. She was taught by the first, who owned a property with a meadow with a stream at the bottom of it. 'What's that for?' she asked him, and he told her 'salmon and trout', so she thought she'd better learn to fish.

He taught her first of all how to fish for trout and she practised on the lawn with a bit of pipe-cleaner on the end of a cast. When she was able to get that onto the saucer he had placed there, he allowed her to go to the river.

She soon became expert, but neither of her husbands were ever jealous of her skills, or worried that she was getting more or bigger fish than them. In fact the first always said that women were much better than men and that they could wade and move

Lady Mallabar applies the pressure. Her best fish from the Welsh Dee scaled 37½ lb.

much more naturally – just as they were better at handling horses.

Lady Mallabar's biggest fish was a 37½-pounder which she hooked in the Slaughter House Pool of the Welsh Dee in 1950. She was with her husband at the time and wasn't going to bother fishing but he persuaded her to have a go. 'Do try,' he said, 'and

Grace Oglesby with summer salmon from the Lune, her first on the fly,
c. 1968. (See page 131.)

The Icelandic Maidens (see page 99). From left to right: Gudrún
Bergmann, Jóna Vigfúsdóttir, Edda Vikar Gudmundsdóttir, Thuridur
Ingimundardóttir, Halldóra ósk Hallgrimsdóttir, Kristin
Steingrimsdóttir, Alfa Hjàlmarsdóttir. (Below) Gudrún Bergmann.

cast over that ridge of rock.' There were lots of bushes around, but she did as she was told, and on the second cast the fish took. She had help at hand of course, and the fish was gaffed before too long. It was the record for the year, 47" long and 27½" girth.

Lady Mallabar was using an old spinning minnow which was very much the worse for wear, but she prefers battered baits. She was using a split cane Hardy rod, as she does now, 40 years later.

Lady Mallabar doesn't like the tailer as a method of landing a fish, but when a net is not practical, she believes the gaff can be efficient. 'If you've played a fish thoroughly, you've got to kill it,' she says, 'so you must do that as quickly as is possible.' And naturally, she puts on her bait or flies herself, although she usually fishes with a gillie.

Her best day was ten fish weighing 160 lb, and there was another day when she got eight and lost two, after which she stopped fishing. All were killed in the Slaughter House Pool, the 10 fish on spinning baits and the eight on a prawn.

MRS JESSIE TYSER

'She fished her water like a man.' This was the formidable Jessie Tyser who accounted for thousands of salmon on her Gordonbush and Balnacoil estates in Sutherland between 1921 and 1970. She was a superb shot and achieved the 'treble' three times: in September, 1926 with a 7 lb salmon, three grouse and a switch weighing 15 stone; ten years later in August 1936 with two salmon, a 13-stone stag and three grouse (not to mention a brace of snipe); and in September 1954, with a 12 lb salmon, another 15-stone switch and four grouse. Dr Lyndsay Laird who worked on the estate for the Atlantic Salmon Trust in 1971 remembers Mrs Tyser as 'very, very fierce'. Failing eyesight had curtailed her angling by this time but there were many stories circulating of large bags falling to her after her guests had retired exhausted. She put fear and trembling into tackle manufacturers at game fairs by insisting on testing their equipment on the spot and she frequently exceeded their claimed casting distances to the consternation of other exhibitors. Mrs Tyser, who was Irish, was a good friend and host to countless sportsmen who could prove themselves worthy of rod and gun, but she never suffered fools gladly and certainly would not tolerate poaching or trespass of any sort on her land.

She didn't ever catch enormous fish, in fact her biggest was a mere 29½-pounder, but her numbers are quite remarkable – three times in Brora she caught 21 in a day and once 22. Rob Wilson who kept the tackle shop in Brora once asked her what her game book total was, and it turned out to be 8,500 salmon! Rob was often invited to fish with Mrs Tyser and he remembered that she much preferred to go for a fish which she knew or *felt* to be there rather than fish blindly down a pool as many anglers do. She had undoubted casting skills and really excelled in upstream dry fly fishing, for which she used an 8'9" Farlow rod which was like a wand in her hands, for she was strong and athletic into old age. Sadly though, she missed out on the carbon revolution and she tended to use the same rods as she got older, but with heavier lines. Mrs Tyser never ate fish and could not bear the smell of salmon.

LADY TRYON

'You never forget your first salmon!' Lady Tryon's was one summer on the Frome in Dorset. It took the fly then headed downstream taking her with it, straight into a bed of nettles! The trouble was that it was a boiling hot day, the sort that every fisher loathes, blazing sun, blue sky, and she was wearing only a T-

Every inch an angler. Lady 'Kanga' Tryon, scourge of the Frome. 'You never forget your first salmon!'

shirt and a pair of shorts. It was a $14\frac{1}{2}$-pounder and put up a good fight, taking her nearly half an hour to bring to the net.

Dale Tryon took up fishing after initiation by her husband and she was delighted to receive a nine-foot, split cane rod for a wedding present. Her husband taught her the rudiments, how to cast, read a river and so on, and Lady Tryon thinks, on reflection, that it's just as well she married a fisher as she loves going over all the details of the day on the river when she gets home. She has lost count now of the number of times she has fallen in. It's partly that her husband is 6'4" and she is 5'6", and a safe crossing place for him is not necessarily so for her – as she has discovered when up to the armpits and swept off her feet trying to follow him.

Fishing for Dale Tryon is the most exciting sport of all, much more so than hunting, shooting or even hang-gliding, and the moment she sees that swirl in the water her heart goes into overdrive. Last light is her favourite time. To step off a plane after a couple of weeks in a rag-trade factory in Hong Kong and get down to the river again is bliss, not just for the fishing itself, but also for the solitude, the ducklings trying to make their way upstream, a water rat going about his business, a kingfisher ...

One of Dale's favourite flies is Hairy Mary, but sometimes she uses flies made from the family's dogs, (labradors and a King Charles spaniel) although the hair from a friend's mongrel has a better texture and swims better.

Lady Tryon is a very busy and jet-setting fashion designer. She started with a modest 16 dresses and now it's over 10,000. So with two *Dale Tryon* collections and two *Kanga* collections a year she has to travel a lot, and she finds fishing immensely therapeutic. She has four children. Zoë is 16, Charles 14, and twins Edward and Victoria 10. Curiously, Edward isn't at all interested in fishing, but Victoria is mad keen. Lady Tryon thinks that lots of fishermen don't encourage their wives to fish because they only have one rod, and frankly they'd rather have the wife sitting on the bank reading.

LILLA ROWCLIFFE

'It's extraordinary the way women seem to catch big fish. I just think we are more careful than men, who seem to lose rather a lot!' says Lilla Rowcliffe, who, although she has been fishing for a comparatively short time, has been remarkably successful, or as she puts it 'terribly lucky!' She caught a 45lb 3oz salmon on the Delagyle beat of the Spey, near Aberlour, and that made her *really* keen. Lilla took up the sport after both her husband and her sister died, as she found herself in a lonely state, and she finds it a great mental relaxation. Now a dedicated fly-fisher, Lilla travels abroad a good deal in pursuit of her passion. When she was in India (for a month, two years running), she tried desperately to catch a big Mahseer (Barbustor) – really the salmon of India – on a fly and eventually after reading a fascinating book on *Angling in India* she went to the Ranganga River in Corbett National Park and caught one – a 35 lb Mahseer on a $2\frac{1}{2}''$ Black Waddington on her 10' trout rod. This, she was told, was the biggest recorded Mahseer caught on a fly since Partition though there was a story circulating that before the war an Englishman got a 90-pounder on a spinner and used the scales as playing cards!

I first heard about Mrs Rowcliffe from the owner of a Borders fishing tackle shop when I had asked about successful lady anglers.

'Well, there's the monkey-shit woman of course,' he said. 'I don't mean to be rude, but that's what she's called, and thereby hangs a tale.'

It was on the River Carvery near Mysore in South India in February 1986, when Lilla was fishing for carnatic carp (they are rather like trout and are found in fast rivers). She was only getting two or three a day at most, couldn't figure out why, but very early one morning with the 'plop' of the droppings of awakening monkeys in the Banyan tree above her tent, the penny dropped too! She duly put on an imitation – a muddler – and caught 21!

Lilla certainly doesn't lack ambition, and is proud to have got

Lilla Rowcliffe. 'It's extraordinary the way women seem to catch big fish.'

a rainbow, brown and brook trout all in one day on the same river. But it took from 9 in the morning until 8.30 pm and the brook trout was last. That was in Argentina and she'd had to walk for three hours, then canoe across the lake to get to the river. She was camping, and found the river very strange, virgin water. Trout sometimes dashed at the fly from under stumps, she didn't think they had ever seen an artificial before. She caught 20 in one day between 2 lb and $3\frac{3}{4}$ lb with two of 5 lb. Lilla Rowcliffe has had other large catches as well, and on a visit to Alaska she got 116 fish in 12 days. 'Quite ridiculous, I'd never go again, it's too easy – but an extraordinary experience.'

She has also fished in New Zealand and Norway, as well as Argentina, where it's all 'catch and release'. And as well as making excellent catches, she has caught her fair share of large fish, too. In the Rio Grande in March 1989 between the 5th and 12th she caught 20 sea trout, including the largest of the week, 18 lb 9 oz, with one of 14 lb, one of $13\frac{1}{4}$ lb and three of 12 lb as well. Lilla's 45 lb 3 oz Spey monster was a cock fish, hooked at 10.30 am on 22 September, 1980, and it took over an hour to land. After the report of this fish in *The Field* there was a correspondence of one or two letters from men who reckoned that they had hooked and lost this very same fish before Lilla landed it.

LADY BRIDGE

Great-great-granddaughter of Flora MacDonald, Helen, Lady Bridge came from a long line of hardy Highlanders, but it was from her father that she inherited her sporting instincts which very early inclined to fishing, though she did shoot, and later became passionate about hunting. Her father rented Muckross, and as a little girl she often proved herself a fearless and sometimes reckless sportswoman around the Lakes of Killarney. One day, regardless of the heavy wind, she rowed herself out alone to troll for trout – a tricky operation for a young girl at the best of times, handling oars as well as rod and line – but nonetheless she hooked and landed a fine trout which at 5 lb turned out to be the largest ever taken on the lakes. Unfortunately, in the process of getting it into the boat one of the triangles of hooks on the spoon got embedded in her finger. There was no one about to shout to for help, and things were looking nasty with a gale blowing on a rocky shore but the child cut the tackle free of the fish with her scissors and rowed triumphantly ashore with her prize, to be rushed off at once to the doctor to have the hooks removed. Next Sunday she was playing the organ as usual in Killarney Church. That wasn't the only time she got herself hooked. On another occasion it was on the tip of her nose with a double hook salmon fly which Lady Bridge left *in situ* by way of bizarre decoration before another visit to the surgery. She was back on the river immediately afterwards and soon caught a fish to console her for the discomforts.

Unusually, it was Lady Bridge who taught her husband to fish, and although she was proud of her pupil he never quite matched her achievements. Sir Frederick was a composer and organist of Westminster Abbey so they had to spend most of the year in London and Lady Bridge wasn't able to indulge in her favourite Spring fishing as much as she would have liked. For some years, though, they took August and September fishing and some shooting on the Deveron, and although she felt that this river was not as exciting as some, it did offer variety and the chance of heavy, fresh-run fish right to the end of the season. Lady Bridge was a great believer in keeping her fly on the water.

She had many stupendous adventures during her fishing career, the most notable of these on the Spean, a rapid and dangerous river which you can only fish from the bank, or wading, in its upper part. The Bridges fished the Spean from 1888 to 1893 and in her best season Lady Bridge landed 43 fish in three weeks, including her largest ever. This was a 43 lb salmon caught on a small mallard-wing fly. Her gillie had told her the fly would be no good and advised her to try a worm, but she refused to stoop so low and persevered with the fly. She hooked the fish wading, in rising and snowy water and since he rose twice before he was hooked she could see just how big he was, which added greatly to the excitement. When hooked (just below the eye) he had to be played for two hours before he could be gaffed, and there was one awful moment when a heavy sleeper from the new Glen Spean Railway came floating down close to Lady Bridge's tight line and she thought she might lose him.

On another memorable evening she landed five fish in two hours (30, 22, 12, 24 and 26 lb) and the last was gaffed by the light of a match. Earlier in the day fish had been rising but not taking and Lady Bridge was convinced that the change of light was the reason and that this has a lot to do with success in salmon and trout fishing.

Helen Bridge was not a tall woman, but she was very strong with wrists like steel. She preferred a greenheart rod to cane for salmon fishing, her reels were of vulcanite (for lightness) and gunmetal, and she fished with a 17 foot or 18 foot rod according to the state of the water, because 'in a strong wind, it is far less labour to fish with a full-sized rod than as some women think, with a light one.' As for the clothing she wore for fishing this is her own description:

> For deep wading I wear the usual trousers, with brogues and socks, and a short skirt of mackintosh, reaching just below the knee, as a cloth skirt gets heavy and hampers one directly it becomes wet. For low water instead of the trousers and brogues, I wear knee-waders, which are boots with waterproof twill tops coming well above the knee,

and a short tweed skirt. Heavy nails are important for all wading, and last better than felt and other appliances. The dress looks neat, and has somewhat the effect of a kilt. Waders are not necessarily dangerous if the wader is careful not to go in strange water where she cannot see the bottom. It is possible to swim in them without difficulty though progress is slow, as I found once on the bank when retreating from a bull!

ROSALIND STAINER

With such a mother it is hardly surprising that Lady Bridge's daughter Rosalind became an expert and similarly intrepid fisher. When she was only eight she hooked and landed (with only a little help from her nurse) a 5 lb grilse on a trout rod. Rosalind fished all her life, usually on the Deveron between Huntly and Glass. In 1954 when she was 70, Mrs Stainer, as she then was, caught a 36 lb salmon singlehanded in St Ann's Pool. She then dragged the fish up to the road (nearly half a mile) to the bus stop where she got on the next bus back to where she was staying.

HILDA MURRAY OF ELIBANK

I doubt if any other sport brings such rest to the mind as fishing. Its very environment tends to this. The music of running water from the gentle, limpid English stream to the fierce roar and swirl of a Highland river, the deep purling notes of the Tweed and other Border streams, or the rippling lights and wavelets of a loch; all conduce to that peace of thought that wipes out time and space, and bears you like driftwood down the flow of hours wrote Hilda Murray in her book *Echoes of Sport*, published in 1910. She was however, a true sportswoman of unequivocal predatory instincts. As a fisher she delighted in studying the river and its pools, and in casting a line so that it obeyed her slightest wish, but if it was to trout fishing that she really gave the palm, luck wedded her to salmon fishing.

Hilda Murray of Elibank, author of 'Echoes of Sport', 1910, in action.

It was as a guest of the Marchioness of Breadalbane of Blackmount (to whom she dedicated her book) that Hilda got her first salmon. Equipped with borrowed 15 foot rod and tackle and all the necessary paraphernalia she found the river in perfect order and managed to cover the pool standing out on the stone jetty. She had on a Jock Scott and had not been casting more than 20 minutes when she heard a splash, then the bump of her heart against her ribs.

> I can feel it all now, at the distance of fifteen years, the rush and swirl of that first salmon, my pulses keeping pace with his runs.

Within ten or twelve minutes she had a nice 15-pounder on the bank, and soon afterwards a second, then from the next pool, a third. Comparing notes over lunch she found that her hostess had had an equally successful morning, and by the end of the day Hilda had five fish and her hostess a fourth, of 27 pounds. It was a record day and guaranteed to make a confirmed fisher of the novice.

After that unforgettable day Hilda Murray took many a salmon out of these same pools, both with fly and worm, and she considered the latter to be the more skilful. But she thought trout fishing a much more delicate and subtle art and not so dependent on a result as salmon fishing where you need the stimulus of success to compensate for the sheer labour and physical exhaustion. Big bags were fashionable in those days and one July picnicking with her friend on the High tops of Blackmount, the two ladies accounted for 15 salmon and 1,000 trout in 10 days.

MARJORIE DOROTHEA FERGUSSON

Marjorie Wisely, as she was before she married Lt. Commander Edmund Fergusson, was another of these formidable pioneering Edwardian ladies with many talents. Born in 1889 she was an accomplished painter of wildlife, an expert on birds, flowers and particularly rocks, had a fine contralto voice and was a superb fisher and a crack shot with a 28 bore. Connections were unsurpassed, certainly from a sporting point of view, and her grand-

*Mrs Fergusson, Queen of the Dionard river in the wilds of NW
Scotland.*

father, Sir Donald Currie, possessed several estates in Scotland.
He had three daughters and bought an estate for each of them,
Garth, Glen Lyon and Chesthill, which belonged to Marjorie's
parents. Sir Donald also owned land on the Isle of Skye, including
the islands of Paabay and Scalpay, and had a luxuriously equipped
steam yacht which was furnished in splendid style, right down to
the stunning Venetian glass goblets which survive to decorate the
mantelpiece of his great-grandson in Perthshire.

Marjorie was given her first rod by her grandfather, and she caught her first salmon at the age of eight. She was a real character and a fervent fisher. Her reputation comes mainly from the River Dionard where the family had a beat and a glance at the Goualinn fishing book for 1955–79 shows consistent success over that period in both river and loch, with salmon, grilse and sea trout. She was 90 when she caught her last fish, and it is said that she jealously guarded her reputation as a superb fisher, and few of her guests would have wished to outdo her.

MARGARET BARTHOLOMEW

Daughter of the distinguished mapmaker John Bartholomew, Maisie, born in 1901, was brought up at Broughton on the Tweed close to John Buchan's family which she knew well. A pioneer skier, mountaineer and motor cyclist, she was a splendid example of the new sporting woman. She studied philosophy at Edinburgh, was a keen shot as well as an expert fisher (hundreds of quails fell to her gun in the Nile Delta), a carpenter and amateur psychologist. Maisie was a singer and talented artist too, had great gifts as a correspondent and also had the temerity to smoke a pipe in public – partly to keep the ferocious Highland midges at bay.

Typically, Maisie was introduced to fishing by the family – three sporting brothers and a tomboy of a sister, and not surprisingly she married a dedicated fisher. The honeymoon needless to say was devoted entirely to fishing in the Scottish Highlands.

'Your eyes are like the wings of a Greenwell Glory,' was the only endearment Margaret Bartholomew could recall ever having been whispered by her husband Hamilton-Grierson, but for someone for whom trout fishing was the ultimate, this must have been praise indeed.

A great beauty as well as a real character, Maisie Bartholomew was not averse to a spot of poaching – indeed she relished it and she also taught her children how to spear salmon using a carving fork tied to a long piece of bamboo. But Maisie was actually less interested in salmon fishing, which she regarded more a matter of luck than skill, than in trout fishing. In this, she was *always* more successful than her husband or other men. So, as a result, latterly the Hamilton-Griersons tended to fish separately to avoid odious comparisons and Mr Hamilton-Grierson *never* invited his wife to join him on his three annual Spring weeks on the upper Don.

Maisie Bartholomew. 'Your eyes are like the wings of a Greenwell Glory,' whispered her husband.

Elsie Wright with 24 lb salmon from the river at Havine Gula, Norway, 1904. Elsie's granddaughter from Edinburgh carries on the feminine fishing tradition.

MARGARET EMMOTT

Margaret Emmott doesn't claim to report any *remarkable* bags. Her best day provided five salmon and none over 20 lb. On two separate occasions though, on the Lune where she lives, and on the Aberdeenshire Dee, she caught fish weighing $26\frac{1}{2}$ lb, the first in February, the second in March. She was alone on both occasions.

When Margaret married a fisherman in 1951 she was offered the choice of a fur coat or some fishing tackle for a wedding present. She got the message, decided anyway that there would be few opportunities to wear a fur coat in the circumstances, opted for the tackle and has enjoyed every minute of the fishing ever since. Margaret usually catches bigger fish than her husband but like most wives puts that down to luck rather than skill, and apart from the two biggest referred to above, she has caught several over 20 pounds.

Mrs Emmott is Editor of the Annual Report of the Lune and Wyre Fishery Association, an advisory and consultative body comprising riparian owners, lessees, netsmen, etc. on the Lune, and of the 25 plus members of the Executive Committee she is the only woman – and of 200 members of the association only three are ladies.

In September 1989, Margaret scored on the Dee, fishing with flies made up obligingly for her by her husband with the badger hair from his old shaving brush. She got 18 fish mostly in the second week, he only got 11 and all the males of the company were duly flabbergasted especially when she told them she was using an old shaving brush.

People talk bluntly in Margaret's part of the world and when she proudly shows her husband a new dress or outfit for a wedding, his response is 'Oh, but I prefer you in your waders.' Her most testing struggle with a fish was at Park on the Dee in March 1985. Fishing alone she hooked a fish in Bakebeare Pool with high water running. The pool is such that the current runs strongly right up to the bank and she just couldn't get the fish in. She decided to walk it down (or rather be walked down by it!) some distance down the river over rough terrain to the Bridge Pool where she knew there was quiet water for beaching. This necessitated wading almost waist deep through a stream. When she arrived safely at the bridge some kind fellow anglers sent their gillie across to help. Margaret beached the fish and he picked it up. It was, by the way, a cold day and her Barbour hood was up. She thanked the gillie profusely and all he could say was, 'My God, it's a woman!'

A few months later the Emmotts were visiting another gillie friend up the valley, who reported the incident of 'the old woman with the big fish at Park Bridge'. 'I was then 57,' says Margaret, 'admittedly with grey hair and not exactly qualifying for glamorous granny, but such is the bluntness of youth! It was a really bonny fish though, 24 lb with sea-lice all over it.'

H.M. QUEEN ELIZABETH THE QUEEN MOTHER

The Queen Mother has been a lifelong devotee of salmon fishing and has enjoyed many a tussle on her favourite river, the Aberdeenshire Dee. She stresses that big fish are not always so lively or exciting in play as their smaller brethren. Queen Elizabeth, in sending us best wishes for the book's success, recalled a great battle she once had with a 28 lb fish which she hooked on the Dee and landed after three hours, three pools further down river.

Wiping Their Eye

ᷟᷝᷜᷟᷞ᷍

'Every man has a secret ambition: to outsmart horses, fish and women.'

Mark Twain

GRACE OGLESBY

Although I have now caught quite a few salmon I don't qualify for a place among those ladies who have caught large fish. My husband Arthur Oglesby usually catches bigger fish than me, but is that not just sheer luck? His present best fish of 49½ lb makes all mine seem like tiddlers; but I have on occasions been encouraged by a gillie to go into a pool behind him and then take a fish to wipe his eye. One memorable occasion came when my husband had to catch a salmon for the TV cameras. I came along and was consigned to a lesser known piece of water where I would be well out of the way. By late afternoon I could see that he was not having any luck and that the camera crew were thinking of calling it a day. It was then that I passed a very small pool – only good for one or two casts, I had been told. Since I still had time to waste I gave it the two requisite casts and just as I was about to reel in I hooked what felt like a small trout. The thought crossed my mind that if I bent the rod into it I could pretend it was a salmon. At that the water erupted and out leapt a beautiful fish. Suddenly the camera crew were galvanised into action; my husband seized the rod from my hands, turned to the camera and said 'The miracle has happened, we have hooked a fish!' He then proceeded to beach the fish for the camera to record.

Occasionally I have the good fortune to catch fish when conditions seem hopeless. It was thus with the first two fish I ever caught on a fly. The Lune was basking under tropical late August sunshine. A few coloured fish skittered about in the deep pools and as I stepped into a bathing suit I told my husband that I was going to practise fly casting. He assured me that fishing would be hopeless anyway. I continued to cast for the best part of half an hour and whether I merely got one so irritated or from some other reason I would not know, but suddenly a salmon took my fly and within ten minutes we had it safely beached. Dismissing it all as a minor miracle, my husband resumed his siesta on the bank. Ten minutes later, after continued casting in the same place, I hooked fish number two which was again successfully beached.

Of course, I realise that such unlikely events are totally unpredictable. There are no absolutes in salmon fishing and the words 'never' and 'always' have no place, but such incidents do my ego a lot of good and make me realise that with a bit of persistence and enthusiasm we can equal the men any day.

LADY GRAHAM

On September 29th [1927] a lady caught two fish weighing 22 and 27 lb respectively. She also hooked and lost, after playing him for quite a long time, another large fish which

Lady Graham with record-breaking brace from the river Aline,
Ardtornish, September 1927. 'Fishing was the great thing for women
in those days.'

would almost certainly have weighed over 20 lb. In any case this was a double record. Two fish weighing over 20 lb have never been caught in one day before and 27 lb is a record fish to be caught on the rod. The previous record was a fish of 25 lb caught in September 1892. Four days later, on October 3rd the same lady caught four fish weighing between 8 and 16 lb.

The extract is from the fishing book at Ardtornish in Morvern on the west coast of Scotland, and 'the lady' was Isobel Sellar, later Lady Graham, who was 17 at the time. There was no special celebration of her record catch on the river (the Aline) which dear family friend John Buchan fished for many years without catching a single salmon. 'Of course stalking was more in John's line,' said Lady Graham, 'and if ever we saw a wounded stag on the hill, we'd say, that'll be one of John's! We girls weren't allowed to use a rifle, so fishing was the great thing for women in those days.'

Lady Graham read history at Oxford and she also played the violin. Her fishing career more or less came to an abrupt end in 1930 when she married the Duke of Montrose and settled in Rhodesia, but she well remembered her youthful angling days. On one occasion she was fishing for sea trout on Loch Arienas with a Dr Blaikie who was writing a book about fishing. She was at one end of the boat, the doctor at the other and two gillies rowing in the middle.

> Strangely enough, the fish kept coming to me, and my companion got rather annoyed, so we turned around, and still the fish happened to come to me!

The doctor duly wrote his book (*I Go a-Fishing*), there is a photograph of young Isobel Sellar in it, but neither she nor her fishing is mentioned in the text. (Lady Graham died 24 August, 1990.)

Billee Chapman Pincher, left-handed caster. 'Men do not like their angling aces trumped.'

BILLEE CHAPMAN PINCHER

> Men do not like their angling aces trumped. They are
> usually more experienced and more expert fishers than we
> are but, perhaps, we are just more fortunate, or maybe
> more patient. I always take longer to fish a pool than my
> husband does and it often pays off.

Billee Chapman Pincher thinks that what ever the reason it needs
to be watched in the interests of marital bliss, and whenever she
catches a salmon prays that her husband will have one when he
comes in. On her first morning fishing in Iceland she was taken
to a pool called the Aquarium and by lunch-time had five salmon.
Fortunately her husband had four and she ended the day with
nine to her husband's seven. Not too flagrant a difference she
thought, but perhaps not to be repeated too often. 'After all, it
is Man that is supposed to be the hunter!'

Billee broke the beat record at Littlecote Fishing Club in '89
with an $8\frac{1}{2}$ lb brown trout caught on a dry fly (the Kennet). She
thinks that women are more delicate in casting for trout, and that
they have more patience in fishing the salmon pools, but puts
down some of her success to luck and to being left-handed, and
therefore covering the water from a different angle following
down after a right-handed fisherman.

MRS WILL FYFFE

The wife of the famous Scots comedian had never fished for
salmon, but on her first attempt landed three fish (25, 24 and
9 lb). It was in April 1933 in Ballathie stretch of the river Tay and
her catch proved to be the record for the season. Her husband
had fished throughout the day and had only managed to produce
a $\frac{3}{4}$ lb trout, but any personal disappointment was mingled with

sheer delight for his wife and by all accounts he was the proudest man in Perth that night:

> Fancy a wee lassie catching and landing a monster like that [he said affectionately that evening]. And that's nothing, she played and landed all three herself, and me, fishing with the same bait, never even got a wee pu'! But, man, I'm fair filled wi' pride, and I've handed over her winnings wi' the best o' pleasure.

Will had promised his wife £20 for her first salmon and they had not been out more than half an hour when Mrs Fyffe's rod (a very light one) took the strain and the reel went 'rattling out grand'. That was the nine-pounder, and as soon as it was landed Will handed over the £20. 'I've never parted in a' my life with twenty quid wi' sae much pleasure but thank goodness I didna promise her 20 pound for every salmon she caught! Really, she's a regular hero, but I'm just wondering how she'll look tomorrow when the terrific strain of landing the 24- and the 25-pounders tells on her arms.'

Will Fyffe had the 24-pound salmon dispatched to London, and the 9-pounder to other friends in England. The largest one was cut up and most of it given to the members of the comedian's party at the theatre. An eternal optimist, Will was back on the river next day to see if he could beat his wife's record – he couldn't.

MRS PEGGY BAKER, MISS VIVIEN BAKER

Burnett (who always wore a Homburg hat), was chauffeur to the Baker family, and until he had driven Mr and Mrs Baker down from London to the Avon, he had never seen a salmon caught. He assumed, quite rightly, that the object of the exercise was to get the fish on the bank as quickly as possible, and he proceeded to do this with a long-handled gaff as soon as any of Mrs Peggy Baker's fish came within range. The water was usually fairly clear, and he would plunge the gaff into the water, the fish sometimes being 3–4 feet below the surface. He never missed. Peggy Baker's two biggest were caught on a prawn one morning in 1936 in High Harbour pool on the Bisterne beat of the Avon, and they weighed 35 and 33 pounds.

The Bakers' daughter Vivien also caught a 30-pounder on a fly in a pool called Okeford Deep, and again the chauffeur whipped it out with his customary zeal. The cast had fallen in a heap in a very contrary wind, but the fish managed to extract the fly from the middle. Vivien meanwhile shouted to her husband that it was only a small pike! Douglas Pilkington, who was married to Vivien Baker at the time, was, and is, also a keen fisher, but he has never managed to beat his former wife's or his mother-in-law's record.

BARBARA HARGREAVES

Barbara Hargreaves was fishing in a boat after lunch on the River Ness with an old friend – a colonel. She had on one of her favourite flies, a Blue Charm she thinks, or perhaps it was a Black Stuart. As it happened, Barbara kept catching fish – five in all – and the colonel got none. What's more the boatman had to keep returning to the bank to land them so it was all slightly embarrassing. Angus, her husband, wasn't exactly euphoric either when he saw Barbara's catch since he hadn't caught any fish himself. But Barbara doesn't believe her success has anything to do with hormones. She thinks women try harder, as they have to in their careers, and if they don't have jobs perhaps they try even harder to achieve results. 'And,' says Barbara, who is very much a career woman, and has had two fisherman husbands, 'frankly, my dear, I have better things to do with my hormones than waste them on catching fish.'

How to Torture Your Husband

PART TWO

THE

SCIENTIFIC

ANGLE

Peter Behan

The Phenomenal Pheromone

'It greatly profiteth the angler to adapt his art to the faculties known to be possessed by the objects of his pursuit. Among these may certainly be reckoned acute vision, sensitive hearing, and the power of discriminating odours.'

Sir Herbert Maxwell, *Post Meridiana*, 1895

'Neurologists have all the best stories.'

William Hartston, *The Independent*, 23 May 1990

Eating behaviour in salmon in general

It has long been known that salmon, when they enter fresh water on their spawning run, do not eat. One of the earliest references to this occurs in a delightful account by the learned professor Hector Boethius, Principal of the University of Aberdeen, whose history of Scotland was published in 1517. Boethius bases his account on observations of salmon in the rivers Don and Dee:

> Finally there is no man knoweth readily where the fish liveth, for never was anything yet found in the bellies other than a thick slimy humour.

Why the salmon does not eat is best explained by evolutionary pressure on its behaviour after returning to spawn in the river.

The salmon has such a voracious appetite that were it to eat, it would eliminate all living inhabitants of a river including its own kin. Why salmon should take the angler's lure and why the taking of this lure can be influenced by different environmental factors is the subject of this chapter. In pure scientific terms we cannot explain why indeed the fish takes a lure. As Hugh Falkus says, the fish's degree of interest varies 'between total disdain and eager acceptance'. Falkus further emphasises what is now regarded as the true situation: 'This implies that there is a variable *reluctance* rather than an anatomical *inability* to feed'. Various theories have been put forward to explain why a salmon will take a lure when his biological status is to be anorexic. The reaction to the fly may be entirely an atavistic one, it may be an aggressive reaction as visualised when large salmon attack small parr, it may even be nothing more than a degree of playfulness or inquisitiveness on the part of the fish. One must realise that in regard to inquisitiveness the fish's only means of examining something that excites his interest is by taking it into his mouth. There may even be a genuine food intake response in a small proportion of salmon whose biological mechanism has not been set at anorexia. The possibility exists that something has occurred to override the anorexic state, allowing the fish back to its sea phase where obviously it is in a feeding mode.

Falkus discusses this in a chapter termed 'Taking Behaviour' in his book on salmon fishing. The point at issue is that salmon generally would not be expected to take a lure because of their anorexic state, they don't eat other fish and their stomachs as described in the 16th century by Hector Boethius are found to be empty. The reason why they take the lure and the various factors that influence this must be of importance in considering why women catch more salmon than men. Before we begin to explore the question further, it might be as well to consider the subject of animal anorexias, or non-feeding modes, in more detail.

Animal Anorexias

Animal anorexias occur in mammals, reptiles and fish and these anorexias are usually associated with certain physiological changes in the life of the animal, such as hibernation, defence of territory or harem (with rearing young or breeding) and in migration where the purpose of the migration is to breed, ie in migrating from a feeding to a breeding habitat. We know that bull seals will starve as they defend their harem and similarly the stag will lose up to 40% of its weight in defending its harem during which time it does not eat. These physiological anorexias obviously must occur as the result of altered appetite mechanisms in the animal. Since hunger in animals has an extraordinary driving force, for the animal to put this aside must mean that there are physiological changes occurring to eliminate the hunger pangs. This is seen during fasting states in hibernating animals such as the ground squirrel when under laboratory conditions it awakes and with plenty of food available does not eat during this latter point of physiological changes. A similar phenomenon is noted in certain incubating birds which can lose up to 20% of their weight during their period of incubation (the capercaillie and the penguin lose even more weight, up to 40% in the latter case). Interestingly these birds will eat but only take about one fifth of the food of a non-incubating sister. The reason why birds lose weight during incubation is not known but it is likely that this weight reduction is biologically advantageous to that particular species. Hibernation by mammals during winter months has an obvious cause, since otherwise many animals might die having expended precious energy in the vain search for food.

Examples of anorexia are found throughout the animal kingdom. Crocodiles fast during the three-month period for hatching their eggs. Whales which migrate from the Bering Sea where the food is rich travel to California to calf. During the migration period and shortly after arriving, they do not eat, indeed like the salmon, their stomachs at autopsy are usually empty. What therefore might be the physiological mechanism that would prevent such animals from eating? While the reason for not eating may be due to evolutionary pressures and for other reasons that would affect the survival of the species around the time of migration, breeding and rearing of the young, there would appear to be a common physiological mechanism occurring in each species where these anorexias occur. Recent work in Scotland carried out by Dr John Thorpe at the Freshwater Fisheries Laboratories at Faskally may help to throw some light on these peculiar animal anorexias. He has observed that the Atlantic salmon, which we know has a period of anorexia in the adult stage during migration, also has a period of anorexia as a juvenile parr. Indeed the interesting finding here is that juvenile Atlantic salmon divide into two populations during their first autumn. These two populations which are readily distinguished by their size have different eating behaviours in that one, the larger group, will continue to eat and migrate to sea the next summer whereas the smaller group may only eat to maintain body weight if at all and will remain in fresh water for at least another year, when at that time they will eat voraciously and go to sea as smolts. It is easy to see the advantage to the salmon of this type of behaviour. It has allowed us to study the brain of these eating and non-eating fish where we observed changes in the hypothalamus.

The hypothalamus is that part of the brain that governs vegetative responses such as sexual activity, aggression, hormonal control and eating and feeding behaviour. Whilst the research is by no means as yet conclusive, there is evidence from our experiments in these fish and other experiments on mammals that certain hormones such as cholecystokinin and neuropeptide-y may have different concentrations in the hypothalamus in the eating and non-eating groups. The theory is therefore that the

anorexic salmon has had the function of its hypothalamus modified which will allow it to ignore food and also explains why it,
usually, ignores the angler's lures. Since later we will show how
the salmon's anorexia can be overcome by certain oral receptor
stimulation and that this reflex is mediated through the hypothalamus, it becomes important to realise that the hypothalamus
is the centre that controls the eating behaviour of the fish. Substances that might in any way alter the setting of this hypothalamic
function would clearly alter the fish's response to eating. This
may be central to our argument later on in understanding why
women catch bigger fish than men, ie the hormonal influence.

Mechanisms involved in salmon eating

VISION The salmon is primarily a visual eater, in other words he
is attracted to his food by sight. This is clearly shown in the
illustration of the salmon's brain where the enormous enlarge-
ment of the optic tectum overshadows all other parts of the brain.
The salmon's brain is apparently composed of three parts, the
biggest dealing with vision, the second dealing with smell (taste)
and the third smaller part dealing with reflexes involved in movement and swimming (and the appreciation of vibrations).
   The salmon being a visual eater, it has extraordinary eyesight.
Examination of the salmon's eye shows that it has both rods and
cones: rods perceive black and white and brightness while cones
perceive colour. Another extraordinary feature of the salmon is
that there is diurnal variation in the usage of cones and rods so
that during the day cones are operative and the fish can perceive
colour but with the coming of night the cones are retracted and
the fish sees only in black and white and predominantly silhouette
form. This great visual acuity will explain the salmon's ability in
turbid or fast running water to see the tiniest fly and to distinguish

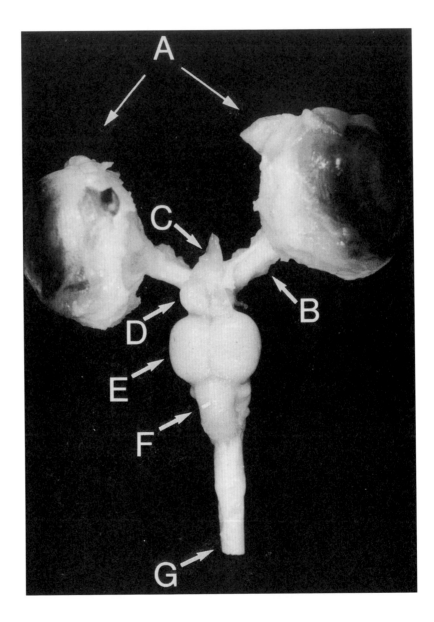

This depicts the dissected head of a salmon. Information from the enormous eyes (A) is transferred via large optic nerves (B) to take part in visual integrated reflexes in the large optic tectum (E). The importance of vision and the amount of the central nervous system given over to visual reflexes in the salmon's brain is obvious. Information from the olfactory epithelium is transmitted via the olfactory nerve into the olfactory area (C & D) where information concerning olfactory data is processed. The cerebellum (F) will help to process information from the lateral line involved with vibration and movement in the fish. The spinal cord is indicated (G). Information from the taste buds, ie the gustatory sense, is conveyed via the 7th, 9th and 10th cranial nerves through the area of the brain underlying the cerebellum (F). Finally, information from the common chemical sense receptors is transmitted to the brain via the 5th cranial nerve to the brain stem beneath the cerebellum (F) and from spinal nerves not shown entering the upper part of the spinal cord and medulla (G).

it from other matter in the water. The rods are essential for the fish in discerning movement and contrast and indeed the salmon is capable of very rapid reaction to movement of an object.

All predatory fish have an inbuilt atavistic reaction to examine anything that moves in their field of vision. Scientists have long known that fish are extremely curious and virtually all fish respond to a certain degree to anything that moves in their environment. One can observe how salmon on the bottom of a river become activated when a worm or shrimp is trotted down near them, irrespective of whether they seize these items or not. Vision therefore plays an extremely important part in the fish's reaction to bait.

SMELL It is often thought that salmon react to a lure only when it comes into their visual field. Whereas this is certainly true of inanimate lures such as flies and spinners, there is no doubt that smell plays an extremely important part in directing salmon to their prey. I have observed salmon in a fresh water loch to be attracted to the discarded entrails of previously caught fish. Indeed once a few salmon began to eat, others were attracted and they too ate and attacked the entrails, including eggs, of a number of their kind as actively as they would have done in a fish farm. Obviously they had been attracted to the material by smell. Other examples show how a salmon is attracted to shrimp and prawn.

I have carried out extensive experiments with whole shrimp and shrimp pieces in fast and slow flowing, shallow and deep rivers containing salmon. There is no doubt that shrimp essence will attract salmon to a bait. Whereas a plastic lure identical to the natural shrimp or prawn may very well catch the odd salmon in a well-stocked pool, the real shrimp will virtually guarantee a salmon at each cast. Clearly there has to be something other than the visual appeal of the bait to account for this and we know that this relates to olfactory stimulation. Fish use both smell and vision to detect food at a distance. Irrespective of whether the fish is predominantly visual, such as salmon, or a chemosensory feeder, such as eel and cod, once the material has been taken in the mouth the composition of the material will decide whether or not the food or lure is swallowed. I will come back to this point presently. Researchers studying feeding stimulants which now have enormous commercial importance for farm-reared fish, have discovered there are certain substances which if added to the bland diet of soya and fish meal will decide whether the food is swallowed or not. The problems known to aquaculturists in farming sole and turbot have been solved to some extent by a scientific analysis of the composition of various foods where it has been shown that the addition of nephrophs or scallop waste to the diet will increase its palatability to the turbot and sole enormously. Initial work done on fish other than salmon has shown extraordinary high sensitivity of the taste receptors to different substances including different amino acids. Salmon have been shown to be particularly fond of shrimp and when purified agar was flavoured with different extracts of shrimp there was no doubt that the salmon preferred an aqueous extract or an alcohol extract of the shrimp but would refuse food which did not contain either an aqueous extract or a methanol fraction. Chemical clues in feeding behaviour are now receiving the attention they deserve. In some species of fish, for example the cod, the specific chemical components are responsible for eliciting various different behaviour patterns used in the detection and identification of food. Salmon on the other hand tend to rely predominantly on vision to detect their prey. Whilst the final acceptance of food is usually determined by taste, smell is important in directing the fish to the source of food as well. I have observed, using a piece of shrimp which could not be identified anatomically as a shrimp, but when placed at the top of a small pool with slow flowing water containing salmon, that the salmon avidly took this material and swallowed it. Clearly chemical clues are important in guiding the fish to the source of prey.

Another and important feature to be understood is what happens when the salmon takes the prey into its mouth. If this is an inanimate object such as a fly or an artificial lure, attempts will be made to spit it out. However, in the case of shrimp and particularly worm, these materials will contain substances that are capable of stimulating receptors on the salmon's tongue and the roof of the mouth. Once these receptors have been stimulated impulses are passed from the mouth to the brain, particularly to various nuclei in the hypothalamus. These stimuli which occur as a matter of a reflex stimulation initiate and programme the fish to swallow. This is an important observation, since every angler who has caught salmon with a worm knows that the worm is sucked and swallowed down into its stomach but only rarely

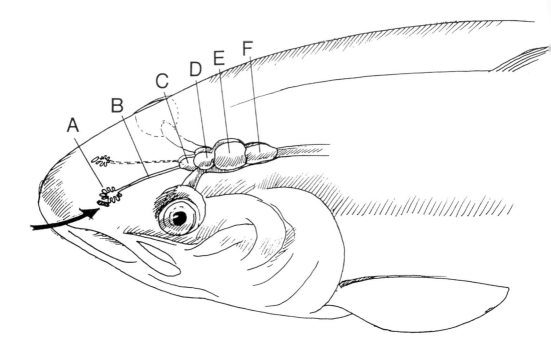

if ever is a lure or a fly swallowed. Worms retrieved from the stomach of a salmon are found to be punctured by the fish's pallatine teeth. This is how the flavour substances are released and the receptors on the tongue stimulated so that the fish is programmed and the material swallowed. Eating therefore in the majority of cases, involves the fish being attracted to the bait by sight, taking the bait into its mouth, chewing it and if the substances contain the appropriate receptor-stimulating flavour such as is found in shrimp, worm or prawn, swallowing. Experiments have been carried out on a variety of fish where electro-physiological recordings have been made from certain nerves and the brain after the fish was given various substances. These substances (e.g. contained in worms and shrimps) that stimulate

This depicts the head of the salmon showing the localisation of the brain and the cranial nerves dealing with olfaction (B) are left intact whilst the other nerves from the floor of the mouth, tongue, gills, gill arches and dorsal fins have been removed for clarity. Water enters the nostril at A which is under control and can be shut or opened by the fish depending on circumstances. The olfactory receptors are dispersed in an ampula (A) and here specialised receptors which are able to detect a molecule of specific substances are situated. These microscopic receptors when stimulated send impulses through the olfactory nerve (B) to those parts of the brain dealing with olfaction (C & D). Such information will be integrated with the visual reflexes which are programmed in the very well developed part of the fish's brain, the optic tectum (B). Data coming from the gill arches, the floor of the mouth, the outside of the surface of the mouth and from the fins will be relayed to the brain stem and spinal cord (F) and integrated with other information in the central nervous system. The specificity of substances capable of stimulating the brain have been tested electrophysiologically by recording from cranial nerves and different parts of the brain when these substances have been introduced through the nasal sac at A under laboratory conditions.

special receptors on the tongue and inside the mouth cause electrical signals to travel to the brain as nerve impulses which can be recorded electrophysiologically. Such impulses (messages) on reaching certain regions of the brain cause the fish to overcome any anorexia and swallow.

Finally fish can also be alerted to the source of prey by vibrations occurring in the water.

We have discussed how the fish takes prey into its mouth. This is predominantly due to the fish being alerted by vision or vibrations to the presence of the object. He will then take it into his mouth and depending whether or not it contains certain substances the material will be swallowed. It should be pointed out that such a mechanism may have little connection with the success of women anglers. Were the water to contain a component that acted on the specialised receptors that salmon have, the fish's behaviour, including its ability to eat, could be modified.

Women Versus Men

We have examined statistics and questionnaires showing the incidence and prevalence of women anglers compared with men. If these statistics show (and they do) that women catch bigger and more male fish than men, then there are several possibilities that should be considered in explaining this documented phenomenon.

1. WOMEN ARE BETTER ANGLERS. There is no data that I know of to show that women are technically better anglers than men. What data exist, come from the observations of gillies and instructors who state that women obey the instructions given to them by the 'experts' and hence fish better. Another feature is that women tend on the whole to be repetitive and fish over a piece of water repeatedly, not exploring or fishing known lies as men anglers do. This may have better results but the data are very vague on this particular aspect. Our correspondent from Oregon, USA, Doc Crawford, puts forward the simplest theory. Doc Crawford has fished most of the Oregon rivers. A lifelong outdoorsman he has worked as a commercial fly-tier, fishing tackle store manager and outdoor writer. He enjoys introducing people to the sport of fishing, and for some years worked as an angling guide. During his years as a guide Doc noticed a curious phenomenon: whenever he took out a husband/wife, boyfriend/girlfriend, or father/daughter pair in his boat, the woman almost invariably caught more and larger fish than the man. It mattered not whether she sat on the right or left side of the boat

nor whether she exchanged places, rods or flies with the man.

He mentioned his observation to Galand Haas, the outfitter he worked for. Galand laughed and said every guide had the same story to tell! And he had a reasonable theory to account for it. Women, he said, are accustomed to being scolded and browbeaten by men; when you tell them to do something in a particular way, they do it exactly as told, to avoid being scolded. Men, on the other hand, feel compelled to show off in front of their women, and prove they are as knowledgeable as the guide, and consequently seldom do exactly what the guide tells them to do. The women, doing exactly what the guide tells them, catch fish, the men, trying to prove how smart they are, catch little or nothing.

2. MEN MAY EMIT SOME REPELLENT SUBSTANCE OR CHEMICAL THAT AFFECTS THE FISH. Many observations have been made, particularly in the north of America where it has long been recognised that the odours associated with the skin of certain mammals can and will arrest the upstream migration of adult salmon. Indeed it has been observed that water rinses of human skin and other animal skin presented to Coho and spring salmon will inhibit the upstream movement for periods of up to 15 minutes following the introduction of dilute solution of these odours. Scientists have observed that on detection of the repellent odour the salmon can be seen to swim excitedly in rapid circling movements away from the offending solution, exhibiting typical alarm reaction. It is extraordinary that estimates show the repellent composes no more than 0.1% of the wet weight of the skin and it has a threshold activity at the dilution of about one part in 80,000 million. This repellent substance is found in the skin of many animals and mammals including seals, sea-lions and other fish but also humans. Experiments carried out on the Clear Water River in Idaho, USA, by our correspondent Mr Garry Hewitt demonstrate the effect of male human substances on salmon. At

the top of a fish ladder where salmon were ascending, Mr Hewitt placed male volunteers and invited them to put their hands in the channelled water. The salmon below immediately retreated from the ladder foot and did not attempt to ascend for a period of 15 minutes following the withdrawal of the human hands at the top of the ladder. The same experiment was repeated with female volunteers. No effect upon the ascending salmon was observed and they continued to swim up the ladder.

As we shall see, fish are capable of discerning an enormous amount of information merely by the chemical messages contained in dilute substances released by one fish and affecting another. These substances have also the effect of inducing strong memory traces so that the effect of the substances will be remembered on the recipient fish.

3. WOMEN HAVE SOME ATTRACTANT SUBSTANCE FOR FISH. There is to our knowledge no definite evidence that women specifically emit a substance attractive to salmon or in some way turn off the feeding inhibition. Such a factor, however, may very well exist as will be discussed under the section on pheromones. What is important is that the so-called 'alarm substance' does not seem to be present in the skin of women and certainly not to the same extent as in men. Secondly women are known to emit pheromones and the possible effect of such pheromones on salmon has yet to be determined. Certainly salmon, as most fishes, react very strongly to chemical stimuli. Their sense of smell is excellent and it is therefore quite possible that salmon could sense the sex hormones of women and be attracted to them. This is a likely hypothesis which has not as yet been proved. Another possibility is that the female sex hormones, or pheromones, could be represented to the fish as pheromones from strangers so that the dominating big salmon go for the smell to attack the imagined intruder. This hypothesis might explain why women often get

the biggest fish and that the record fish they catch are predominantly male. There are now some extraordinary facts known about the olfactory system and the perception by fish of chemical messengers, ie pheromones. Pheromones operate at several stages in fish behaviour, including species recognition, sexual function, dominance, schooling, attraction to food and the presence of predators. These chemical signals, pheromones, are substances which are secreted by one animal and are perceived by a second animal, usually of the same species in which they effect a specific behaviour reaction. They are usually divided into two, namely releaser and primer effects. The releaser pheromones trigger a rapid, acute response in another individual, this usually being of a stimulatory role, whereas the primer effects alter the physiology of the fish through the endocrine system so that the animal may affect or display different behavioural reactions in the future.

Since fish live in water, communication by chemicals would seem to be extremely important to them and have a pivotal role in their survival, growth, reproductive success and other physiological and biological functions. These pheromones in fish are perceived through the sense of smell or taste. One of the most likely effects of such pheromones is to reveal the presence and location of food and of predators. As stated such pheromones as have been found in fish of different types usually have a stimulatory role and act very quickly. Fish in deep water at night when the water is coloured will depend to a large extent on this chemical type of communication. Originally the existence of such chemical signals was demonstrated by Carl von Frisch 40 years ago, but it is only recently that a study of chemical communication in fish has been taken up very seriously. So far experimenters have not been able in the majority of cases to differentiate between smell and taste pheromones and their effect on alerting the fish to food. However, these pheromones have enormously important behavioural actions, such as the control of migration within rivers and estuaries, survival value in detecting predators, sexual attractants and also aggressive responses which have been measured in the absence of other cues. The distinctive taste (or flavour) of the home stream is imprinted in the young salmon and it is this remembered chemical pheromone that is so specific that allows the fish to find the river where it was born. There clearly also may be cross reaction of pheromones from one type of fish to another whilst they may be entirely species specific for another. For example the fright reaction is not species specific – one type of fish may react to the alarm substance emitted by other fish – but the intensity of the response is related to the phylogenetic proximity of the species. Again the sexual pheromone has been demonstrated to be highly specific even among closely related species such as the blennies (a spiny sea fish) where an exact specific pheromone is necessary for breeding. A lot of present data suggests that these pheromones in fish may to a large extent be related to sex hormones and steroids and aliphatic acids. These latter substances have been shown to be extremely important in olfactory behaviour of fish. Bile salts which are composed of these substances have the greatest potency over any other olfactory stimulant known to fish. As stated by Doving 'the odourant potency of the bile acids, their evolutionary history and variability, together with their renowned adherent properties, make them interesting candidates for specific signals in aquatic environments.' Bile acids can adhere to virtually anything and bile from the gall-bladder of the trout can produce responses in other fish at a dilution of 1 in 1,000 million. Bile salts' main function in the vertebrate body is to help with digestion. They adhere readily to most substances and their chemistry is related to hormones.

The exquisite sensitivity of chemical languages in fish has been examined particularly in catfish. Catfish not only react to pheromones to help them find prey and direct them towards food, but they are able to distinguish dominant and non-dominant members of the family entirely on the pheromone each of these species produces. It has been shown that pheromones from such fish involved in fights are capable of communicating to other fish the winners and losers in bouts for dominance.

Pheromones

A pheromone is a chemical that one animal releases and that another animal smells; the pheromone induces changes in the behaviour of the second animal. These chemical messengers are extremely important in animal behaviour and have been shown to operate in animals and lower forms, particularly reptiles, insects and fish. The pheromone may act in two ways; by immediately eliciting a response in the second individual or by inducing some reaction that may result in chronic endogenous changes in the second animal. This second type of behaviour may take hours or days to become effective. Since the lower forms rely much more heavily on the sense of smell than humans do these pheromones have important physiological roles. Examples of their function are that they allow the animal to recognise its own species, to differentiate male from female and to recognise when a female is in heat. Pheromones can also have some other effects, eg the pheromones released by female mice can affect another mouse's oestrus and the odour of a male mouse can also have extraordinary effects on the oestrous cycles of female mice. So strong are these effects that it is known that the odour of a male mouse may cause a pregnant female mouse to abort. There have been several claims that humans produce pheromones and that these pheromones may have important behavioural effects. It has long been recognised that women confined together, for example, in a boarding school or convent, may have synchronisation of their menstrual periods. Indeed women produce pheromones which arc similar chemically to those of monkeys. These fatty acids are produced in the greatest amounts around the time of the middle of the menstrual cycle when oestrogen levels are highest and when the probability of becoming pregnant is also greatest. It is known that oral contraceptives have an effect on these pheromones.

Species reactions are common, eg humans react to the smell of musk whereas bulls, monkeys and goats may be affected by the odour of women. We know that in humans there are organs for which no function has been ascribed but were they to be found in other mammals would be readily recognised as part of the pheromone system. These include special glands associated with hair tufts. Patterns of response in humans are also interesting since it is known that women have the greatest sensitivity in detecting odour which is oestrogen dependent, eg women react to certain smells more readily than men. However, scientists have not paid as much attention to the chemical analysis of these substances in humans as has been carried out in the case of insects and lower forms. Interestingly most, if not all, of the pheromones in humans and in mammals are derived from fatty acids, ie steroids. Most mammalian pheromones are contained in the urine although special secretions are produced by the sex glands through the skin including through the axilliary exocrine glands. We know that odorous steroids are rapidly transferred to objects handled by pregnant women through the sweat.

Whereas man may have lost his dependence on smells for sexual communication and social interaction, primates still are dependent to a very high degree on olfactory mechanisms in communication between the sexes. Such pheromones are import-ant in their social organisation. Male Rhesus monkeys made incapable of smelling do not react to females. Indeed the chemical nature of these substances which are highest in the secretions from female monkeys have been analysed and shown to be short chain aliphatic acids. Indeed a synthetic mixture of different acids such as acetic, propionic, isobutric, isovalcric and isocabroic acids have the same effect as the naturally occurring pheromones. The identification of these sexual pheromones in the monkeys as simple aliphatic acids shows that in the order of mammals below man pheromones have powerful behavioural effects. Similar type action of pheromones is thought in humans to induce the menstrual synchrony referred to above. There are many reports of this menstrual synchrony in the literature. One example was where seven female life guards were separated at the beginning of the summer. After three months living together again all seven had cycles which fell within a four-day period.

The exquisite sensitivity of smell is seen in animals such as dogs. This has long been known in their ability to track human individuals dependent entirely on their scent and in their ability to distinguish between non-identical twins but not identical twins. This phenomenon of the olfactory system which has such exquisite sensitivity and is so specific, rivalling even classic neurotransmitter receptors in the brain, has only recently received close attention from scientists. There are olfactory receptors which are soluble rather than membrane-associated in the olfactory epithelium of the nose. On contact with the specific substance or pheromone binding occurs and the receptor transmits messages to the brain. These impulses are transmitted to the oldest part of the brain, namely the limbic system, the part that deals with primitive emotions and behaviour such as sexual function and appetite. It is therefore readily appreciated how stimulation occurring in this way can affect emotional behaviour responses.

It has long been recognised that of all animals fish have an exceptional need to be able to establish communication through chemical, ie pheromone, messengers. These messengers affect their social life, their eating, reproduction, schooling and even control dominance. How important olfaction is to fish is readily observed when one looks at the size of the olfactory lobes in the brain. In the salmon one can observe that the two biggest parts of the brain deal with smell and vision. In some species the area for smell dominates the sensory side of the nervous system and even overshadows that for vision. This olfactory sense has exquisite sensitivity and specificity. Molecules of a substance are enough to stimulate and affect behaviour in fish. Associated with smell in the salmon and other fish is the function of taste. Interesting experiments have been carried out on fish that have been blinded. These fish are capable upon being introduced to small amounts of water from tanks containing other fish of showing behavioural responses depending on the chemical messengers present. For example, if two catfish fight and one is removed and placed in a separate tank and water from the tank where the fighting occurred introduced to the second tank the fish in that tank will go into a frenzy. If water is taken from the tank of a non-fighting fish and introduced to another tank, the recipients will be activated to curiosity but not to fight. This shows that different behaviours are transmitted via chemical signals. Water taken from the tank where two fish display courtship behaviour can have the effect of sexual arousal on a fish in another tank. These patterns of behaviour in fish which have been demonstrated to occur via chemical messengers, ie pheromones, do not occur in the recipient fish if the olfactory system is damaged. Only when new olfactory tissue has been regenerated does such behaviour occur. The pheromones are given off by various tissues but most of them are found in the mucus of the fish's skin. It has been suggested that pheromones from the mucus of the skin will help another fish to identify the species whilst odour from the gonads will identify the sex. Similarly it has been suggested that the pheromones from the urine of a fish may tell the recipient whether the first fish is a dominant or subordinate individual.

Pheromones almost certainly are involved in the homing of the adult salmon to the rivers in which they were born. This theory put forward in the 19th century has been subjected to scientific analysis. We know that salmon return from the sea to spawn in the particular stream or tributary in which they began life. Experiments on salmon in which the ability to smell was suppressed have given some support to this idea that pheromones guided the migrating fish. In one study salmon had an electroencephalogram, their brains wired to an encephalographic apparatus, and were infused by different water from different sources. When water from some rivers was infused through their olfactory sac no change occurred in the electroencephalographic recordings. However, when water from the river in which they were bred was introduced it produced a significant response.

Further observations on different fish have shown that pheromones are important in the recognition of males and females. We know that females from a wide variety of fish including trout are attracted to the odour of mature males of the same species. In the case of pheromones here they are usually of a stimulatory role. Females were strongly attracted to water that had previously held ripe males or to water taken downstream of spawning trout. Pheromones released by the female act rapidly in the male, causing an increase in sexual activity and attracting the male into the area from which the pheromone is released. It is therefore clear that chemical signals – pheromones – play an important role in communication between fish and in relationship to social order, dominance, aggression, sexual activity and in attracting the fish towards food.

The pheromones have been shown as stated to be most important in allowing the fish to migrate homewards after their sojourn in the sea. Those from the salmon are thought to be released from the mucus of their skin and several experiments have shown that when young fish are conditioned to pheromones from one area and released there they return to that particular area. Professor Doving studying this phenomenon in Norway has stated 'The results of the experiments carried out have strengthened our belief that population-specific odours make the trail that the salmon follow back home, that the odours come from the fish itself and that if the fishes "memorise" the flavour of the rivers, it must be these specific substances.'

The question therefore is whether human pheromones or other substances might have an effect on fish. We do not know for certain whether this can occur but there is anecdotal evidence to suggest that it may. Pheromones from humans may affect other species as already mentioned. In silkworm culture over many centuries in India, Japan and China the cultivators of these worms have evolved certain customs, which if not complied with, deter the worms from producing silk. From the hatched worms all smells are removed since these can affect them. The attendants are required to be absolutely clean, must wear simple clothes and are not allowed to eat chicory. The women are forbidden to smoke, use modern make-up or eat garlic. It is interesting that whilst these customs are strictly adhered to among the silkworkers in China, in Nigeria too, the Yoruba women employed in the gumming of the silk are forbidden to cohabit with their husbands. Similarly the men who look after the silkworms in India are expected to stick to a vegetarian diet and are not allowed to shave or cut their hair nor are they allowed to cohabit with their wives since this is thought to interfere with the silkworms' progress. Since a female moth can give off pheromones in a single burst that attract males from a distance of eight miles it is not inconceivable that these ancient customs are based on practical observations of the deleterious effects of odours on the sensitive silkworm.

Apart from the Clear Water River, Idaho, it has also been reported from several other rivers that the scent of male human skin can have an alarming effect on salmon. Indeed it has long been believed that the secretions of human skin induce fright reactions in salmon and other fish. Many river trout anglers of the old school used to rub their hands in earth or even cow manure before baiting their hooks, to mask the human scent. Whilst such deterrent substances exist and are claimed to exist in males, other substances may have highly attractive properties for salmon. Two such substances are taurine and sulphate conjugates of bile acids. They are highly potent olfactory stimuli. Certain amino acids are also highly stimulatory. And indeed a large number of studies have shown that salmon are even more sensitive to some of the bile acids than to the amino acids. It has previously been shown that amino acids have been the most potent group of olfactory stimuli for fish in general. Norwegian scientists have now demonstrated that bile acid derivatives are even more potent than amino acids or any other group of substances examined. They explained this high sensitivity to the bile acids 'as a specific sensitivity to this particular configuration'. They state, 'Thus in the olfactory receptors there must be acceptor sites specifically designed to react to the bile acid derivatives'. Furthermore they showed that this sensitivity in salmon varied throughout the season.

Summary

It is a commonplace that women are good anglers and catch bigger and more salmon than men. The reasons for this are unknown, but we have discussed the possibility that they may be better technical anglers and that men may repel fish, particularly as observed in experiments in Northern America. To give women the edge over males in achievement the possibility exists that they may somehow through chemical messengers affect the salmon's taking behaviour. This last statement, whilst still lacking scientific confirmation, may not be as extraordinary as it actually seems. Chemical communication with exquisite degrees of sensitivity and specificity exists in fish. Social communication has been established among fish. There is a role of chemical communication for dominance, aggression and sexual behaviour. All of these phenomena are communicated through their chemical senses and fish clearly can detect in the water chemical substances in very minute quantities. Experimenters have found that fish possess an almost incredible chemosensory acuity. For example, the great Professor Teichmann was able to study eels and show that they responded to concentrations of alcohol which were so dilute that the animal's smelling ability was able to detect single molecules of the substance. Detailed physiological studies of catfish in captivity and of other fish have shown that they use their sense of chemical communication for many biological purposes and that the behaviour of the fish such as schooling, dominance, aggression, fighting, sexual activity and feeding are exquisitely controlled by chemical signals. For example, some chemicals can cause a fish to stop fighting, others to initiate attacks and inquisitiveness. Hence, it is entirely possible that pheromones from women may bring about some of these effects, particularly in male fish. It is known that dominant male fish may set up and establish a territory that they defend against intruders and since they will detect intruders not only by sight but by chemical communication, one can readily see how a bait or a lure put into the area of one of these large fish so stimulate it to attack.

Finally, the idea, however exotic, that women may influence salmon so that they catch large, male fish still may have a scientific basis. Certainly, no one would claim that all of the fish that women catch are due to a unique phenomenon, but rather that at times they may somehow be helped by chemoreception and this may explain their success. Smell in salmon is rooted to the olfactory bulb in the brain and is used primarily for social communication and is of little use in foraging. This is new data but takes into account recent physiological studies on fish. The sensory modality commonly linked to foraging is taste and there are two gustatory subsystems: one from taste buds on the general body surface in front of the mouth which projects to a certain part of the brain and is responsible for locating a food source in the environment. There is yet another system which activates taste buds at the back of the mouth and from the gill arches. This system is critical for the fish to evaluate the item it has taken into its mouth and whether it should be swallowed. However, only very recently has yet another chemosensory system been discovered which holds particular promise for our idea of how women may affect salmon through sensory chemical substances. Single specialised cells with unique physiological properties have been found to exist in the skin of fish. Some of these cells have unique physiological properties in that they respond exclusively to very complex stimuli and not to basic amino acids or sugars. These cells respond extremely well to chemicals contained for example in urine and particularly in human saliva and also in the mucus of other fish. The idea therefore is that a chemical as yet unknown, but probably hormonal, is transmitted to the water by handling of the rod or handling of the lure. This is detected by such cells. How the bait is attacked whether as an aggressive act or as a food mechanism, or an inquisitive phenomenon awaits to be proved.

These ideas are new and have not so far been tested scientifically, although scientists in a number of university laboratories are now looking at the possibility that substances from mammals, including humans, may be able to have an effect on fish. These ideas we have put forward mainly to try and explain the observed facts and future scientific work will be required to see if there is any truth in such suggestions.

THE LAST WORD

JANE WRIGHT
(*Fishing instructor*)

Men do feel they are the dominant sex, they think perhaps they can dominate women, and they think they can dominate fish – and if they think that, they are in for a cruel awakening!

EDDIE McCARTHY
(*River Superintendent on the River Thurso*)

Women are much more attentive, and 90% easier to teach than men, what's more, they retain what they have been taught better than men do. But women have a very strong competitive spirit and they want to outdo the men, probably because most men don't take them seriously ... Men can be very rude about lady fishers behind their backs too, you should hear them in the bar! but the ladies are consistently successful and there was one week in particular, on the Thurso, in April 1987 which is memorable. Twenty-eight fish were caught that week, 26 by the ladies of the party and two only by the men – and those on the Saturday.

Index

References to illustrations are given in italic.

PICTURE CREDITS

The authors acknowledge with thanks the loan of family photographs from private collections reproduced in this book. For the use of copyright photographs acknowledgement is made to the following: Hugh Falkus, page 4; Richard Allan, facing page 17; Perth Museum, pages 31 and 64; The Hulton-Deutsch Collection, page 48; H. F. & G. Witherby Ltd, page 57; Arthur Oglesby, page 72 and facing page 112; Gudrún Bergmann, facing page 113; John Wolstenholme, page 135.